The
SILENT
Agreement

AN ILLUSION of INCLUSION
in BLACK CORPORATE AMERICA

HOW to FIGHT
with CONVICTION
and
AVOID BROKEN PROMISES

Wil Shelton

ISBN: 978-1-7368613-0-1 (Paperback)
ISBN: 978-1-7368613-1-8 (Ebook)

Library of Congress Control Number: 2021910284

Editors: Wil Power Marketing Services

Cover & Interior Design: Juan Roberts / Creative Lunacy

PUBLISHED BY:

Publisher of Nonfiction Business Books
14742 Beach Blvd. #163
La Mirada, CA 90638
www.wilpowermarketing.com

Printed in the United States of America

CONTENTS

Suppose you've never had a conversation with Wil Shelton one on one; well, here is your chance. Reading the **Silent Agreement** will give you life and give you a mental workout unlike you've ever had. Each chapter works with another different muscle in your brain. If you've ever felt that corporate America doesn't understand, value, or even appreciate your journey as a person of color. Then this book is for you. My advice is to stretch before you read this book because Wil will not take it easy on you or your feelings.

—Keni Thacker
Founder / Chief Creative Officer
Roses From Concrete

FOREWORD

*"**IF** there is no struggle there is no progress. ...Power concedes nothing without a demand. It never did and never will."*
—Fredrick Douglass, 1857

We have been trying to hold a conversation about diversity and inclusion when in actuality, we are in a fight to reach real diversity and inclusion. Wil Shelton draws this out by tying the struggle to achieve inclusion to a boxing match.

All fights are not physical, but that doesn't mean we are not fighting anyway. Wil highlights how our desire to obtain diversity has us in a fight that we have not fully committed to winning, but we can if we shift our mindset from having a conversation to winning a mental boxing match.

You are going to be uncomfortable reading this book. Good. That is the beginning of growth and evolution. To become more inclusive, we have to fight with how we think about others and ourselves, we have to fight to change the systems, policies and practices we have put in place to prevent us from changing.

Reading this book may hit you in your feelings and cause you to sway a little but do not let it knock you out. Keep bobbing and weaving. Learn how to take a punch as well as give one. Most of all, understand that we are fighting for change, not having a conversation. Put your mental gloves on and let's get at it.

Derek Walker, CEO
Browner and Browner Advertising

DING, DING. ROUND ONE.

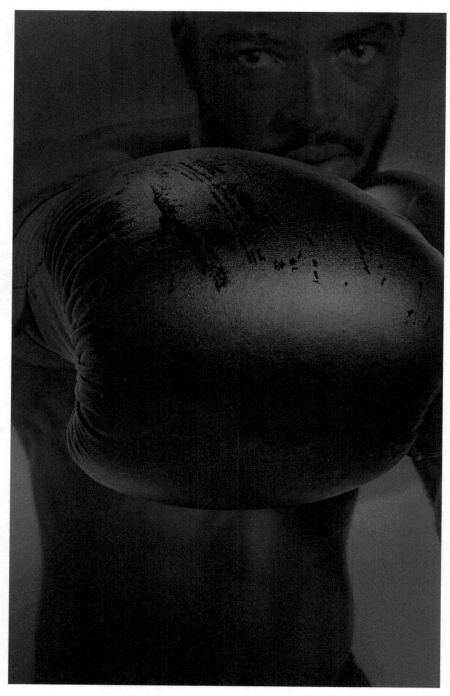

ROUND 1

Putting on the
GLOVES

IN the early eighties, a street-hardened, 16-year-old kid named Michael Gerard Tyson was left in the legal care of his boxing manager and trainer Gus D'Amato after his single mother died. At that time, Tyson trained at the Catskill Boxing Club where Teddy Atlas assisted D'Amato in molding a young Tyson into the fearsome heavyweight champion he later became. D'Amato and Atlas helped Tyson perfect his signature "peak-a-boo" style of boxing in which he quickly slips his head out of range of his opponent and moves it from side to side to remain elusive while setting up his offense. Skills like this are what make boxing so fascinating to watch.

Remembering back to those early training sessions, Atlas once said of Tyson, "We used to have to pay sparring partners because he punched so hard that he knocked them out. Then every so often we'd get one that he couldn't knock out." When the latter happened, Tyson engaged in the "silent agreement" in which he would lean against his also-exhausted opponent giving both of them a chance to rest. Atlas blamed Tyson's habit of making this agreement as immaturity, and he told Tyson to stop doing it. Atlas said to Tyson, "Stop making silent agreements. Because one day you'll get a guy who won't sign a contract."

As a competitive weightlifter, athlete, and business owner, I've often thought about the correlations between sports and the fight for racial equity within corporate America. Specifically, I've noticed that Black executives inadvertently make silent agreements to be content with less, to not fight for what they deserve, and to fully support the demands of the corporate administration even when those demands conflict with their own community, culture, and conscious. Those who comply with these unwritten contracts with corporate America almost always find out the hard way that the other side hasn't signed. Even though African-Americans may stay silent about the day-to-day racism they experience, and they may even help ensure other Blacks stay on the "Black track" (the path that inevitably leads toward a managerial plateau), they are never rewarded. In fact, they come to feel like psychological contortionists who are betraying their true selves and their own culture to further what they think are their future interests, but with no real payoff.

Research conducted by McGill University's Patricia Faison Hewlin shows that many minorities feel pressured to create "facades of conformity," suppressing their personal values, views, and attributes to fit in with organizational ones. As Hewlin and her colleague Anna-Maria Broomes found in various industries and corporate settings, African Americans create these facades more frequently than other minority groups and feel the inauthenticity more deeply.

The major disconnect for Black men and women in corporate America is that they experience racism and micro-aggressions in the workplace every day, even as they are told that "everyone" is on board to combat these corporate conflicts. Many times, when Blacks point out race-related problems, they are punished in ways large and small by white group-think that seems to say, "We knew you would cause problems. We're letting you be here. Isn't that enough?" A noted psychiatrist once summed it up this way: "Those

Black executives in the potentially greatest psychological trouble are the ones who try to deny their ethnicity by trying to be least Black—in effect, trying to be white psychologically."

These futile attempts to blend in play out in corporations across America, as Black men and women who are tired of battling micro-aggressions and flagrant discrimination at work simply make a silent agreement to stop fighting. Even those who don't completely stop fighting still don't fight with the same intensity they once did. Instead, they start throwing "don't-hit-me" punches, because they are no longer trying to win, just mentally survive while waiting for the conflict to be over. Many promising Black executives leave corporate America altogether once they understand that they will never be able to win the ultimate prize: access to corporate C-suites and boardrooms.

An unfortunate majority of African American executives accept that they will be relegated to positions in race relations, community relations, or public relations while never being given opportunities to serve in meaningful positions in marketing, operations, finance, or information technology. This is not a coincidence. It is a construct of predominantly white senior corporate boards and senior executives who excuse their racism by saying that Blacks are not qualified, not the right fit, lack the right personality, or countless other frustrating reasons designed to obscure the truth: They do not want to African Americans in their ranks.

AS OF THIS WRITING

- Fewer than 10% of senior executives that operate business units are African American.[5]

- Just 3.3% of all executive or senior leadership roles are held by African Americans.[6]

- Approximately 1% of board members in the S&P 500 are African American.[7]

- 37% of boards do not have a single Black member, according to an analysis by Black Enterprise magazine.[7]

- Fewer than 1% of Fortune 500 CEOs are Black.[8]

- Only 3 African American women have led Fortune 500 companies (SHRM, 2021).

Exclusionary tactics within corporate environments have had a devastating impact on the progress of Black America, and, ironically, have resulted in a huge loss of talent and innovation, immeasurable in its depth and breadth. Yet, while many African Americans choose to make a silent agreement after years of throwing powerless punches, this does not mean the fight is over.

After Mike Tyson stopped making silent agreements, he went on to be the undefeated heavyweight champion from 1987 until 1990 when he stepped into the ring against James (Buster) Douglas on a Sunday in Tokyo and reverted to past behaviors.

Commenting on the fight in which Tyson allowed Douglas to tie up his hands in clinches, Atlas said, "It was a silent contract. A free ride for the opponent, who often was glad to have it. This time, Douglas didn't go along with the silent contract. He punched and made Tyson come up with something different." Douglas knocked Tyson out in ten rounds, taking his title as he did.

African American executives cannot afford to make the same mistake. Like boxing, winning in corporate America is as much a mental fight as it is physical. It is imperative to understand the tactics used by corporate America to keep African-Americans down and fight with conviction, blow for blow, without making silent agreements that are bound to be broken.

WISDOM TO APPLY IN
THE CORPORATE RING:

• "Stop making silent agreements. Because one day you'll get a guy who won't sign a contract." — Teddy Atlas

• "Those Black executives in the potentially greatest psychological trouble are the ones who try to deny their ethnicity by trying to be least Black—in effect, trying to be white psychologically."

• Like boxing, winning in corporate America is as much a mental fight as it is physical. It is imperative to understand the tactics used by corporate America to keep African-Americans down and fight with conviction, blow for blow, without making silent agreements

BOXING STRATEGY

GO TO THE BODY

If you feel outmatched by an opponent, taking body shots will help wear them down. Head shots are predictable and easier to avoid, while body shots lower an opponent's guard and brings his or her eyes down, making it easier to set up a head shot.

Beating the
BLACK SCORECARD

RECENTLY, the Covid-19 pandemic and simultaneous Black Lives Matter protests have shined a light on the -economic boxing ring in which African Americans find themselves doing battle every day. Though it may feel like a new battle, the match-up between Blacks and corporate America has always been an unfair fight. From the very beginning, those who are in positions to judge the abilities and acceptability of Black Americans have used a different scorecard than they would for white Americans— one that is weighted with stereotypes about what does and does not represent Eurocentric ideals of appearance, manners, work ethics, speech patterns, cultural cues, and more. Clearly this scorecard is weighted in favor of whites, and therefore the Black scorecard puts African Americans at a deficit, even as children.

Nothing about this double standard is new to African Americans. From the time they are little, Black children are told by their parents that they must be twice as good at everything to get a portion of what they deserve, because even when they are more qualified and outperform their white peers, there are people who will actively work to steal victory from their hands just to see them fail. For this reason, it's instilled in Blacks that they must always punch above their weight class to get ahead, and once they do, they can't ever punch down because they know how quickly they can fall.

The never seen but always present Black scorecard also means that young Black professionals spend as much time training for conflict and survival than training for success. This is especially true for Black men and women who dream of being decision- makers within a corporation, because even when they out-achieve their peers while performing psychological contortionism to fit into the white executive mold, they may still find that they are only candidates for the Black track. For instance, urban initiatives within major companies have been used for decades to keep African American workers in particular segments of a company and away from the mainstream work and opportunities. John P., for example, might be made the vice president of urban sales rather than a vice president of sales simply because of his race. This is not a compliment; it is another river to cross, a subjugation and career suppression in its most subtle form. According to the Harvard Business Review article *A Dream Deferred*, "the psychological contract made by corporations is unfulfilled for Black high achievers. We're dealing with a breach of contract."

Above and beyond the need to fight harder for every win, Blacks are now faced with new challenges. Currently, the world is mired in a global pandemic and facing economic uncertainty and political instability, and the United States is reeling from unprecedented blows to healthcare, the demise of the business sector, public safety, racial equality, and democracy itself. These blows have landed squarely on the chins of African American men and women who are more likely to contract and die from Covid-19 and more likely to sustain crippling economic injury due to related business restrictions or loss of employment. The latter is often the result of opportunity after opportunity lost to the Black scorecard. No matter how hard Black men and women fight to get ahead, the judge gives the points to the other side. There is not always one discernible knockout that can be seen and commented on by onlookers. No, in this ring, Black fighters are simply expected to keep fighting for fewer points until they are exhausted or knock themselves out to end the fight.

How corporations hire, train, and promote African Americans has a lot to do with this dynamic. An Associated Press analysis of government statistics found that white workers have a better chance than Black workers of succeeding in job categories with the highest median annual salaries. The ratio of white-to-Black workers is about 10-to-1 in management, 8-to-1 in computers and mathematics, 12-to-1 in law, and 7-to-1 in education, compared with a ratio of 5.5 white workers for every Black one in all jobs nationally. Behind corporate walls, they may attribute this to poor education, a lack of interest, or a poor work ethic. Many corporate leaders claim that they simply cannot find the Black talent to even the game. This form of racism is akin to gaslighting, in that it puts the onus back on Black hopefuls, requiring them to work harder to prove themselves.

Watch any news program, and it's clear that America is still a nation gripped by racism. The current social hierarchy and powers-that-be ruling over the American success story continue to promote Eurocentric, so-called American perspectives that specifically exclude African Americans and others of color. This cultural game-fixing has not impacted all races equally. Many other people of color such as Asians, Latinos, and Native Americans have been brought into the C-suite circle faster and more consistently for years as the U.S. becomes more diverse and hiring practices are put under the microscope, but one could argue that positive stereotyping and lighter skin tones make it easier for them to blend in. Racism against African Americans is so deeply entrenched in American culture that the rules at play are specifically designed to exclude them first and foremost.

This strategic offensive against African Americans has led to two classes of Black executives. The first group will kowtow and submit to loaded offers of auxiliary, secondary, or symbolic C-suite positions versus fighting for positions that would empower them to influence the direction and future of their companies. The second group may try and fail to beat the system, after which they ultimately resign from the struggle, choosing instead to create their own companies or work for Black-owned businesses that give them a fighting chance.

Inevitably, both groups of Black executives will most likely work for organizations that fail to represent them personally or culturally, even when those companies claim to be committed to inclusiveness. The stated goal of such companies is something akin to E Pluribus Unum, "Out of many, one." However, when the 'many'—or the broad spectrum of Black perspectives, values, and interests—are not favorably represented, the "one" continues to act as a largely homogenous echo chamber of white voices. By undermining Black representation in corporate America, backward-thinking C-suite and senior executives undermine their stated values, the profitability and growth of the corporations where they work, and the American economy itself.

Though many corporations are beginning to give public lip-service to Black Lives Matter and the current sociopolitical realities of the U.S. regarding police brutality, police shootings involving African American victims, inhumane conditions for offenders, and excessive sentencing of African Americans, claims of solidarity with the Black community mean little when no major wave of hiring Black C-suite executives has taken place.

To be clear, no one is proposing that C-suite positions should simply be handed to unqualified Black executives; only that the same scorecard is used when evaluating their performance. This would be game-changing for Black executives that have been passed over time and time again for subtle and not-so-subtle reasons related to their race.

On the flip side of those waiting patiently for their chance to rise within corporate America, there have been many successful Black executives who refuse to accept a rigged fight and instead power forward with fervor, honor, and stability much like a prize fighter. They are entrepreneurs, moving like free agents, but often they don't have the financial resources that large competing corporations have, which still puts them at a disadvantage. In short, the fight is always rigged.

What's needed is a game plan for companies who seek to make the fight fair for everyone they hire by addressing and supporting discrepancies in representation within their organizations. There is a clear need to respond to the questions Black executives have and address the survival strategies they use before they feel forced to choose between submitting to the Silent Agreement or leaving corporate America altogether. Ultimately, this will provide Blacks with a third choice in which there is a payoff for battling in the ring. There must be an incentive for Blacks to fight their way up the corporate ladder—and how they are scored should follow the same rules that white executives play by: Fair fight, winner take all!

A standard set of rules and a referee make boxing more competitive by leveling the playing field so raw talent and grit are the only things that matter, and any man or woman who fights hard enough can win. This open-ended competitiveness raises the bar on talent and builds a larger audience in the process—something corporate America should pay attention to.

When Black consumers invest in corporations, they expect a reciprocal investment in the Black perspective. Often, they are disappointed because for corporations to fulfill their end of the bargain, they have to invest in African American talent in marketing, sales, operations, budgeting, and outreach, the very departments traditionally dominated by whites. If corporations want to build their audience while raising the bar on talent, they should promote Black executives to these relevant C-suite positions where they will be able to represent their culture and be champions of their communities.

A lot has been said here about what corporate leaders should do differently, but they are not the only ones who must rethink their behavior. Black executives and administrators must also refuse to make Silent Agreements or accept the Black scorecard. All too often, African Americans retreat from potentially confrontational scenarios in which they know they are right because they are afraid to rock the corporate boat, but in doing nothing, they simply defeat themselves. The "good ole boys" system was designed to instill a mentality of appeasement among African Americans who trust their personal sacrifices will ensure professional advantages and financial gain. So where is the prize? If they were thrown into a boxing ring, would these same men and women be content to take punches and only throw a few to keep the other fighter off of them or would they strive to win? If the answer is the former, why fight at all?

Historically, African Americans are fighters. Against all odds, we have successfully fought through inhumane subjugation to win our own freedom, we have fought racially motivated intimidation, humiliation, and violence to win the right of inclusion. Now we must fight against unspoken boundaries such as the Black scorecard and Black track to win our rightful place at the corporate table.

When Black executives accept token positions or participate in empty discussions about multiculturalism, inclusion, and enfranchisement all the while knowing that the true goal is maintaining the status quo, we are defeating ourselves. Many Black executives are content to do a song and dance to avoid raising race-related questions, but this only benefits whites who don't want to talk about Black issues because it threatens their advantage.

But let's TALK ABOUT IT.

The reality is that African Americans represent 13.4% of the U.S. population and have nearly $1.5 trillion in spending power, yet only 0.8% of Fortune 500 CEO executives are African American (currently five men, and no women). Furthermore, African Americans represent just 3.2% of all senior executive positions (Brooks, 2019).

These are the outcomes when the Black scorecard is used to call the fight. It enables misinformation, a lack of solid agreements, and often blatant acts of sabotage by the white majority of C-suite executives to continue. African Americans cannot show their true worth when points are being deducted for the color of their skin and underperformers do not share a voice in the corporation—even when that underperformance is a mirage.

The Silent Agreements made by Black executives are indicative of how deeply they accept the role of being "less than." When their experiences or communication styles do not align with those of white colleagues, they often submit and accept the call that it is a deficit on their part rather than a difference in culture, education, and upbringing—a difference that can bring untold value to the corporation. Black executives often allow themselves to be sidelined, taking full body punches while hitting back with meager jabs, such as requesting multicultural sensitivity training.

The fear of delivering a punch to the status quo that may end in all-out war, makes it nearly impossible for Blacks to openly share their feelings, insights, or questions with white colleagues. They also know that if they continue bumping heads and trading punches with executive management or the administration, they risk being marked as 'difficult'. Then later they may be marked as at-risk for demotion or termination.

But why should Black executives simply be quiet, docile,

and at the will of the senior executives and the board of directors? Black executives represent the future of American consumerism and can help heal the tenuous relationship between Black consumers and American companies. Sometimes companies fail to solidify Black support because they are unaware that the fight is fixed or that their best fighters are never even allowed to enter the ring. Increasing the level of support for Black executives can bring more talent to the table, which will ultimately drive greater profitability.

Other corporations know they should be doing more, but it is easier to talk about it than to take action. But even if corporations can't do what is best out of an authentic sense of altruism, they can look at the dollars to make sense of why they need to uplift deserving, hardworking individuals who are currently being held back for being assertive, innovative, insightful, and Black.

The need for more African Americans in C-suite positions couldn't be greater. In a time where Blackness is being attacked by conservatives; Republicans are tainted with Trump's mode of operation; and white supremacists and police abuse the civil rights of African Americans, corporations and their allegiances have an opportunity to be heroes.

Although, there is an American concept of separating church

28

and state, business brings these two forces together. With business comes politics; this cannot be avoided. Business reflects the state of politics, both overt and underlying, and, at this time, business leadership reflects both overt and covert forms of racism that unapologetically impede the progress of Black executive development and growth in C-suite leadership. Yet workplace racism does more than hold Black America back economically; it holds back the corporations that myopically cling to erroneous and outdated notions of African American leaders being somehow unequal, less complex, and far more chaotic than white leaders. How can they authentically connect with new and valuable demographics when they fail to understand the people who represent them?

Black consumers demand authenticity in marketing, which requires corporations to understand the vast range of Black perspectives nationwide. White executives trying to figure out what Black people are thinking and placing a few Black faces in advertisements or on the board doesn't work when actual Black voices are muzzled or the spectrum of African American needs go unrecognized and unmet. American corporations benefit when Black C-suite executives are helping to lead the charge from key positions within marketing, operations, management, and even budgeting. But too many corporate leaders feel that such an investment is precarious and threatens the loss of sociopolitical opponents of Black equality. It is reported that Caucasians make up 74% of the American population, so many devalue African Americans as a small minority. However, with increasing incorporation of white Hispanic/Latinos, white Amerasians, North Africans, West, Central, and South Asians who can easily pass as white, this percentage may be inflated, and census organizations stand as some of the most racist institutions that shape the economic, financial, and sociopolitical futures of African Americans in this country.

Ironically, even despite the obvious benefits of checking the white box in America, the vast majority of Americans still turn to African Americans for cues on what's cool. America has always followed Black America's lead when it comes to fashion, entertainment, and even attitude, because it is in stark contrast to the white stereotypes of the stuffy Northeasterner, the brooding farmer from the Heartland, the sassy, spirited Southerner, or artistic yet seemingly lackadaisical extrovert from the West.

In all regions of the United States, whites have borrowed liberally from Black culture in one way or the other, even those who eat their barbecue with pride while listening to Elvis and Johnny Cash. Even proud racists appropriate Black culture and assimilate it into their cultural definition of what it means to be American. However, focusing on the fashion, appearance, and overall stereotypical aspects of Blackness has further excluded Black people as an integral culture in the very fabric of the American reality. Without Black people, America as we know it would not exist. Again, Blacks are natural-born leaders and their ideas are often innovative. So why are so few heading American corporations?

Again, the problem lies with the Black scorecard and how whites award points for assertiveness. white assertiveness is seen as an asset to the corporation, while Black assertiveness is seen as aggression. For instance, when a Black executive steps on white toes to get a job done, those are not just any toes. White toes are on the path to the C-suite by default and stepping on them will quickly become a stumbling block to the Black executive. The unspoken message is that if a Black executive needs to step on toes, those toes better be Black.

Yes, it's still true that crabs in a barrel is the best metaphor for how some lead Black executives keep their jobs. They are no different than the Black overseer who was enslaved but ready to punish and destroy any Black assertiveness to appease the slave master. Historically, turning Blacks against Blacks is a technique used to keep them all in check.

This legacy of self-hatred and self-doubt in the Black community is alive and well, and it is one of the most difficult obstacles for African American executives to overcome. Therefore, it is the rebel, the maverick, the Black man or woman in a position of power that is willing to take blows and punch back at the barrage of institutional harassment and social intimidation that white, lead executives practice to maintain "business as usual." They do this by keeping a scorecard of their own, ensuring that any action or environment that does not align with corporate equity policies is recorded and validated and that Black concerns are quickly addressed to ensure that policies reflect the needs of all stakeholders.

There are two sides to empowering Black executives to act as diplomats that can help rewrite the scorecard and incorporate African American culture and values. On one hand, there is a need for a speaker that can represent and unite the differing viewpoints of African Americans, Caribbean Americans, American Africans, and Afro-Europeans. These various cultural groups need representation and a liaison to maintain a positive dialogue with big corporate America. But this ideal scenario rarely exists because Black interests have yet to be fully incorporated as a norm in the American business scheme.

The other side of the Black executive diplomat—the downside of such an honor—is much more prevalent. It involves being a puppet of white interests and exploiting Black dollars, values, and influence for no other reasons than to capitalize on trends. In this role, Black executives validate the Black scorecard and ensure that it is applied every time Black assertiveness rears its head.

On the other hand, Black executives can take the lead with a plan to promote Black culture and leave a legacy. Representative John Lewis, politician and civil rights activist, is one such Black leader. He once said that he met 'good trouble' with assertive, proactive, and decisive strategy. His legacy still stands as a means to strengthen the progress of Black executives in politics and the private sector.

Simply playing along and making the Silent Agreement to

appease exclusive, traditional interests of the white Corporate hierarchy is foolish at best, but it has been a survival technique of many Black executives for years. In many ways, it is a fight or flight response when conflict is at hand. At times, there are clear opportunities for Black professionals to become relevant C-suite executives, yet they may feel ill-received by certain members of the leading administration, which prevents them from taking such a giant step in their career. They would rather focus on compiling further proof of their value to solidify their place in the company than risk rejection at the highest levels. This should be recognized for what it is. Blacks do not linger in low-level positions out of job satisfaction or loyalty, but out of fear—the fear of failure and the consequences that follow. Even in the smallest business, failure for Black professionals know that failure will not only cast a shadow on their reputation but on their racial demographic as a whole. In short, Black men and women aren't in the ring alone—they are always fighting for a larger cause, and sometimes the prize is not worth the risk of losing.

Black executives are faced with a host of losing propositions. They must accept the Black scorecard and be a Black-track executive, fight the system and risk everything, or throw in the towel and leave. In addition to this dilemma of deciding on a path forward,

Black executives are fending off a barrage of overt and covert microaggressions exchanged when their white contemporaries challenge Black authority or knowhow. Eventually, the tension builds and their fight or flight instinct kicks in. Some deny this is happening and choose to flounder and simply bear the pressure while holding onto a hollow, symbolic position. Often it comes down to pride vs. denial. Pride will make a person lose his or her job, but denial will keep it. Though denying that you are being disrespected, ignored, overlooked, and taken for granted is more sacrifice than the job position is worth, it requires less maneuvering and minimizes conflict. But by sacrificing pride in Blackness, Black executives undermine the accomplishments and aspirations of other Black professionals who are set on expanding and enriching corporate America from the C-suite.

It is denial that leads so many Black executives to sacrifice self-respect and respect of the communities from which they came. These Black executives fail to best represent and speak on the needs, challenges, and interests of Black people in America from consumers, employees, or members of surrounding communities. They don't mind being asked to the party but are never asked to dance. They are happy to sit on the sidelines and watch white executives dominate the C-suite dance floor.

On the other hand, those Black executives seeking to make a mark for themselves are only there because *they want to dance*. For them, anything less is failure. It is time corporations stopped inviting African Americans to the party to act as props or spectators and started asking them to dance. Better yet, why not ask them to lead or even choose the dance? Only when this happens will true change have occurred.

Unfortunately, African Americans have not seen enough Black prize-fighters in the corporate arena. Most have only witnessed vague scenarios where a few Black men and women share in American endeavors for national growth, whether it was commercial, social advocacy, or even a military endeavor. One example is General Russel L. Honoré, a leader in charge of safety, planning, salvage and rescue during Hurricane Katrina. Honoré made life-changing decisions regarding how to effectively administer immediate medical care, food, clothes, and shelter during a national crisis.

At face value, American politicians, members of the military, and law enforcement agents can point to Honoré as an example of Black leadership, but the exception proves the rule. Though Honoré is an honorable man and a historically recognized leader, he is not the norm, whether he was working as a public servant or executive of private interests. The need for incorporation includes greater, deeper amounts of inclusion by making the very beliefs of differing people the norm as a foundation for the performance of future generations of African Americans.

The images of Black people and Black culture shape not only the perspective of Blacks by others of color and those of whites, but the imagery impacts how African Americans see themselves in comparison to others regardless of race. Historically, imagery in advertising mass produced grotesque caricatures of African Americans that were predominantly rooted in racism toward men, women, children, old, young, light-skinned, and dark-skinned. It didn't matter. Nevertheless, the imagery stuck until the present moment. In 2020, there was finally a long overdue abandonment of the Aunt Jemima logo which presented a cartoonish and deplorable 'mammy' image. Still, the image of Aunt Jemima was based on an actual enslaved, older African American woman, Nancy Green, who had been chained to tables and stoves and forced to cook meals before and during the Civil War. A century later, the horrific story of Green's life and the exploitation of her image associated with Black servitude as a precedent in white American culture was diluted and rebranded to sell pancakes and maple syrup.

Throughout history, images of African Americans have been synonymous with drama, fantasy, and commercialization. The racist notions that shape America's image of Black America were communicated through a white lens, such as was the case with D.W. Griffith's 1915 film, *The Birth of a Nation*, which featured a South devoid of Union soldiers to keep the peace. In the film, free Negroes roam the countryside for no other purpose than to attack virginal, Christian white women. Who saves the day other than the Ku Klux Klan? Unfortunately, the film celebrated the underlying sentiments of many whites at the time. President Woodrow Wilson had the film screened in the White House and praised it for what he deemed as an artistic and accurate depiction of recent history. The celebration of such propaganda was devastating because it led to even greater investment in racist images and storylines across generations of cartoons, movies, music, theater, television shows, news media, and later social media.

Corporate America also has roots in slavery, racism, and even police brutality against African Americans. Regardless of how many PSAs and tweets corporations release, until their administrations, management teams, and team leads reflect inclusion that is more favorable to African American interests and stability, their carefully crafted words remain hollow, and their motivation appears solely to continue exploitation versus incorporation of African American talent and the Black dollar. Meanwhile, they continue to judge Black employees against the Black scorecard.

Much like General Honoré, there is always an elite among African American leaders, activists, performers, or businesspeople such as Oprah Winfrey, Tyler Perry, Shawn "Jay-Z" Carter, and Dr. Cornell West. Such people are held up by both advocates and opponents of greater Black achievement and administration. Both allies and enemies of greater African American influence hold the success among African Americans as proof that racial minorities ("minorities" being another code-word rooted in prejudice against African Americans) are exceling at a rate comparable to that of the white population. The one-off successes of African Americans in business, entertainment, and politics including the military, are used to disprove racial disparities in leadership, financial gain, and the quality of life.

Yet, the reality is that African Americans remain a minority consciously limited by whites with a traditional mentality of what Black success should look like. It should never be too common, too great, or too liberated. The fear among a majority of conservatives and many liberal whites is that Black leadership will only benefit African Americans and exclude Caucasians. In other words, they are afraid that what they have done to Blacks will be done to them. This fear upholds a hierarchy that is the foundation of racial disenfranchisement and marginalization. Whites are set on remaining in power manipulate the system to ensure that the concerns, futures, and the very existence of non-whites remain on the periphery.

Instead of the constant waste of funds and resources on lip service and empty words that demand action, corporations who claim they share solidarity with Black lives and Black causes must be willing to reform their scorecard by ensuring that key performance indicators or KPIs reflect a commitment to equality, civil rights, and diversity-based efforts. These corporations must be willing to be assessed by joint groups of government and private organizations in collaboration under the leadership of Black executive members. The assessment for these corporations would be a 100 to 150-point inspection that assesses specific areas such as operations, financial management/budgeting, administration, manufacturing, community outreach, partners, vendors, ecological impact, diversity, ethics and compliance, and corporate image. The entire organizational structure, function and current outcomes, as well as the organizational culture must undergo evaluation to essentially establish for corporations when whether or not their claims of support for Black lives and advancement are valid. In other words, those corporations need to put their money where their mouths are or stop wasting their breath.

Authenticity of corporations and their support of Black lives must go beyond the endgame of maintaining Black dollars flowing into annual revenues, generating those market-ranking profits so many brands strive for. The protests led by notable organizations such as Black Lives Matter have taken place in nearly 2,000 locations nationwide in response to police shootings and murders of unarmed African Americans, which has generated public response from leading brands such as Target, Ben and Jerry's and NIKE. Yet, until further development, the words of support and solidarity from these brands only serve as an acknowledgment of socio-economic hurdles that they themselves do nothing about. Now, it's a matter of "put up or shut up." If such companies not only refuse to share their statistics regarding the diversity of representation within their C-suite administration but also refuse to practice what they preach and they do not promote a significant number of Black executives, their words are puffs of polluted air.

There is clear evidence that Black representation among corporate leadership is lacking and demands that hiring practices of these so-called companies united with the Black cause fall in line with the reality of American demographics, politics, and social conflicts. In order to fall in line with needed hiring representation, such corporations should maintain a C-suite administration that is 13% African American or higher. These Black C-suite members must be placed in positions overlooking marketing, sales, branding, operations, finances, procurement, human resources, and other key areas of corporate power versus the stereotypical placement of Black executives solely in the urban department or as leaders of diversity and inclusion.

It is sensible on the part of corporations to place more Black executives in meaningful C-suite positions in order to reduce errone-ous, corporate-propagated micro-aggressions, historical race-rooted obstacles that undermine advancement and impede stringent African American representation at the corporate table. Former CBS Diver-sity Manager, Whitney Davis, made it clear that big money corporate America will only sell the idea of being an open, inclusive institution when that association offers advantages for the company regarding consumer interest and profits. Corporations will smile holding the doors open for Blacks who will be satisfied with low-level or man-agerial jobs, but access to the top floor, the leadership, the brains of the operation is denied to even the most accomplished profes-sional solely because he or she is Black. The psychological effects on the Black executive mind have been equated with being robbed at gunpoint, but in this case, American corporations rob Black executives of time, skill, determination, and expertise, leaving them empty-handed and often feeling like they have less when they decide to leave such companies for better professional and personal opportunity (Bradley, 2019).

Whitney Davis shared shocking stories of how she was confused with another Black woman by white executives, who revealed their racist notions, essentially telling Davis, "You all look the same..." Davis further stressed that even as a diversity manager for a major television network, she still ran across stiff resistance that translated into a toxic combination of racism and sexism. When Davis stated that she was interested in joining the programming team, the head of programming, a white male, simply stated there were no positions available. He provided no means to mentor, groom, or potentially recruit Davis to any position in his department. Instead, the programming head selected a far less skilled or complex personality to join his team. He picked a mediocre-performing white male instead of Davis, a Black woman. To add insult to injury, the same mediocre white man continues to rise in the ranks at CBS (Bradley, 2019).

Why would a major corporation like CBS allow mediocrity to lead simply based on race and gender? White men are roughly 35% of the nationwide population, so what, other than racism and sexism, would lead corporate leaders to let 35% of the population decide what is best for all of the differing perspectives among the general population? Companies that believe that 35% of the population should be speaking for and making decisions on behalf of the other 65%, are lacking in innovation, vision, and common corporate sense when it comes to customer retention, corporate image, and branding enriched by incorporating a broader spectrum of clientele.

Even though less than 20% of white Americans are blatantly racist against African Americans, there are over 50% whose actions may be observed as neutral, thus supporting the blatant racist actions by the lesser percentage. By not speaking out, not objecting, not valuing the defense of Black interests, this neutral group is supporting racism. As Black Lives Matters protests continue to shine a light on systemic, racist tactics such as the Black scorecard, corporations that claim to stand with Black America can no longer hide behind neutrality. It is time for them to reimagine the boxing ring of corporate achievement so that it includes fair rules and objective referees. If they don't, they may soon find that the consumer scorecard is stacked against them and that their tradition of fancy footwork, slick maneuvers, and double-dealing is no longer enough to defend their titles from the coming backlash.

WISDOM TO APPLY IN
THE CORPORATE RING:

• From the very beginning, those who are in positions to judge the abilities and acceptability of Black Americans have used a different scorecard than they would for white Americans—one that is weighted with stereotypes about what does and does not represent Eurocentric ideals of appearance, manners, work ethics, speech patterns, cultural cues, and more.

• No matter how hard Black men and women fight to get ahead, the judge gives the points to the other side. There is not always one discernible knockout that can be seen and commented on by onlookers. No, in this ring, Black fighters are simply expected to keep fighting for fewer points until they are exhausted or knock themselves out to end the fight.

• There must be an incentive for Blacks to fight their way up the corporate ladder—and how they are scored should follow the same rules that white executives play by: Fair fight, winner take all!

- If corporations want to build their audience while raising the bar on talent, they should promote Black executives to these relevant C-suite positions where they will be able to represent their culture and be champions of their communities.

- Instead of the constant waste of funds and resources on lip service and empty words that demand action, corporations who claim they share solidarity with Black lives and Black causes must be willing to reform their scorecard by ensuring that key performance indicators or KPIs reflect a commitment to equality, civil rights, and diversity-based efforts.

"

Sometimes our greatest strengths become our greatest weaknesses.

"

BOXING STRATEGY

DON'T TOUCH GLOVES

Boxers normally touch gloves with their opponents before the first bell and after the last bell as a sign of respect. When you're forced to fight harder for every win, not touching gloves with your opponent can be intimidating. It says you mean business, and you have no intention of throwing don't-hit-me punches or playing nice.

Don't-Hit-Me
PUNCHES

WHEN boxers get into an exchange but notice they are either being outmatched or they are simply failing in strength, speed, and precision, they panic. Instead of covering up and maintaining balance as they move and get off the ropes or timing their opponent's blows before lashing out to strike, many boxers throw don't-hit-me punches. Imagine seeing boxers who don't want to get hit——don't want to fight——throwing wild, random punches like a schoolyard kid in a wild tantrum of tears. Sometimes children who fight by windmilling their arms win; other times, windmilling fails, and a kid hits the floor or blacktop flat on their face. Whether they are fighting a bully or they themselves are the bully, children who resort to windmilling will always lose at some point. The same goes for the boxer who snaps, loses sight of the strategy needed, and neglects to use fighting techniques (defensive and offensive) that will win the fight. Instead, these boxers focus solely on not getting hit, which scares them into pulling punches, throwing a random Hail Mary of blows, or grasping their opponent in an attempt to stop the opponent from swinging.

Black executives most often find themselves in similar scenarios when they are under pressure to perform. They know they are at a disadvantage because many of their white, traditionalist colleagues expect them to fail. This expectation may not be overtly communicated but it is entrenched in a system of institutional racism reinforcing an unspoken pecking order that places Black executives at the bottom. To avoid exacerbating this dynamic, when conflict arises about a product, advertisement, or policy, a Black executive may sidestep to stay out of the fray and diffuse the intensity of emotions. Black executives may even resort to changing their demeanor, tone, eye contact, and overall wording in an effort to lower the temperature in the room by better regulating how he or she is perceived. But why should Black executives have to silence themselves or curb their emotions and words for the sake of the status quo?

Some white traditionalists already look at Black colleagues as inferiors who made it into their roles based solely on affirmative action, but the truth is that most people who benefit from affirmative action are actually white women (Massie, 2016). The skewed perspective of white traditionalists may be unfounded, but they are still effective at marginalizing African Americans and their progression within corporate America. Many Black executives feel daily pressure to choose between career-shifting reprimands or kowtowing to oppositional white executives.

When white executives exhibit assertiveness—or even aggression—in the workplace, they are applauded as passionate, robust, and revolutionary. African Americans can have ideas that are all of these things, but they are read as threatening. Black executives are often undermined, discredited, or rebuked for their standpoint because their white superiors are looking through a discriminatory lens. White traditionalist executive members rarely recognize or admit that this difference is racially motivated. Rather, they see Black ideas as a force that can threaten the foundation of the business, its networks, and, ultimately what they perceive as success from a traditionalist (racist) perspective.

Black people have been in America working as long as white people, even if the origins of that arrangement were far from ideal. Unfortunately, Black professionals who believe they are working within a more current American society, thinking that we should be beyond the racist dynamics of yesterday, too often find that their troubles are here to stay. Though the song did not refer to civil unrest and racism stretching through time, reflecting on the Beatles' song "Yesterday" (1965) seems appropriately applied with some poetic license to the present day. Black people are eternally fighting the same opponent within the American corporate machine—not just when they work in the kitchen or engine room, but even when they are at the helm of a department or overseeing a team of their own. They know from experience that this opponent fights dirty and hits hard. When they are reprimanded for speaking up, it can be a career-endangering blow. In a panic, Blacks may throw a series of don't-hit-me punches to save face but with no strategy in mind. This constant cycle is exhausting and depletes the energy they need to keep fighting.

An example of throwing don't-hit-me punches in the corporate setting is arguing over company policy and how it is applied. For instance, it is a policy of corporations to be more inclusive if they want to expand their customer base or to focus on a market segment and address their needs. One need is the need for visual representation. Black customers have been vocal about wanting to see African Americans in the commercials of brands in which they invest. Corporations frequently support casting biracial children with darker Black parents. This is not blatant racism, but a subliminal message that somehow dark-skinned children are not as attractive as those who have significant European ancestry. Such subliminal messages are considered detrimental to communities of color regarding how they perceive their self-images.

Members of the Black community who are aware of this travesty of Blackness often take up social advocacy to protest brands that still use such racialized marketing tactics. But instead of a number of white executives taking heed of the obvious mistake or blatant disregard for cultural sensitivities, they continue to defend racialized marketing that promotes colorism within the Black community. The obvious undertone to this stance is that "White is right," and the closer one is to the European standard of beauty, the more attractive they are.

Of course, white traditionalists and apologists use deflection when their ruse is revealed. Later, many of them will try to coerce the Black executive to stop the argument through essentially trying to buy the Black executive off or use intimidation regarding the Black executive's job future. If the Black executive takes the pay off, basically he or she is bought and considered to be on the traditionalist's proverbial ticket; therefore, the Black executive is no longer a threat to the continued abuses of Black images and influence in American marketing by the white corporate establishment. Essentially, that's taking a punch in the face but later growing weary and giving in to the opponent.

If the Black executive continues to push their opinion on this racially charged issue, the white traditionalist could switch from being defensive to becoming accusatory. Suddenly the Black executive is overly sensitive and projecting divisive, anti-white bias onto innocent images of African Americans. The truth is that Black people have insight into how imagery can elevate or distort African American culture, and that insight is a strength for the corporation. Caucasians do not have any such reference point or experience. They are not privy to certain nuances in Black communities and base their understanding on representation that is commercialized and therefore accepted as the cultural norm. But if those norms do not actually reflect values of the Black community, then products and services based on the false norms fail to meet the needs of the intended market segment. Nevertheless, in the given marketing scenario, white traditionalist executives will continue to pressure the Black executive until he or she submits, decides to quit, or requests a transfer.

In this scenario, the Black executive is fighting in the best interest of the corporation, and yet because he or she is throwing don't-hit-me punches, the result is the status quo wins out and the executive is worn farther down, unsure whether or not the fight is even worth it. The real tragedy is Black executives experiencing such racially-motivated theatrical reprimands are simply trying to create more inclusive communications that reflect the needs and desires of the customer. It's business, but prejudice and ignorance make it personal. And, unfortunately, white executives can punch below the belt without penalty.

If the Black executive in this argument is willing to concede defeat, the white executives, practicing rituals of socialization, will remind the Black executive that he or she should feel honored to be involved in the decision-making at all and he or she is a credit (an exception) to their race. In fact, Black executives often find themselves being paid or afforded limited power for their silence on critical issues that often don't just affect African Americans; they affect the very people discriminating against them (i.e. products containing harmful chemicals or side effects for any consumer). The Black executive accepting a token assignment or position for his or her submission and silence is like a boxer clinging to his or her opponent because he or she doesn't want to risk being hit.

Like these Black executives, some boxers become risk-averse, throwing punches only when they know they can score. They may put up great numbers, but you never really feel like they dominated. Instead of going for the knockout they leave it in the judges' hands. But fighting not to lose means one lacks the strategy, precision, and focus to win.

Fighting to win comes with more confident, heavier, and more precise punches. Weak punches are thrown from a lack of confidence. In the end, it's a matter of fear. The fear of being hit comes from the belief that one will not be able to counter and stop the opponent, even when throwing formidable punches. Fear-based fighting relies on defensive moves that prevent the fighter from exposing themselves to opportunities for the opponent to take advantage. The same consideration exists in war, strategic conflicts, sports (of course), and especially corporate America.

Sometimes our greatest strengths also become our greatest weaknesses. African Americans have become masters of defense. We may use every defensive tactic we can think of to stay in the ring, but this hinders us from digging deeper, believing in ourselves and going for the knock-out when there is a clear opportunity to take it. There are usually many instances in a Black executive's corporate career when they have been in a position to end fights early, if only they were willing to step up and take the risks necessary, and yet they don't. This is like Michael Jordan stopping short of taking a shot when the game is on the line in the finals to win the Eastern conference finals championship or if Serena Williams stopped using her serve for fear of double-faulting. Both boxers and Black executives must operate with flexibility, dexterity, and uncompromising confidence to win.

One way for Black executives to gain this confidence is by building his or her own network through committees and collabo-rations as well as social interest groups with influential members of the organizational infrastructure. Black executives that have allies and resources can curb the impact of white executives who pose opposition solely based on underlying racist notions of the American workforce established along classist, racist, and sexist lines.

The problem is that Black executive allies may be external to the organizations with little influence on the internal decisions, functions, or outcomes that take place. Corporations themselves should work toward providing those internal allies to prevent Black executives from feeling beat down and fearful of going toe-to-toe again, because if Black executives don't conquer their fears, they are like boxers who fail to stand their ground. They end up ceding all the power they were given when they were hired.

When a Black executive begins to anticipate potential conflict, how they'll be set up, the arsenal that will be used against them, and the outcome the opposition wants, that's pressure unlike any other. Having internal allies is like having a trainer who can objectively anticipate the punches an opponent will throw. This trainer can help the executive anticipate oncoming attacks and avoid wasting energy and losing the will to win.

For instance, Black executives are often charged with participating in diversity and inclusion programs, yet they are guided by traditionalist, white executives on how to deliberate and delegate within that realm. A company committed to diversity has to make D&I part of its DNA. An authentic diversity and inclusion program cannot be overseen by those who historically started the "bs" – biased situation-- in the first place. That's like having a diversity group formed by female employees, but only including women who are approved by men. Women's equality organizations, specifically in areas of equal pay and administration, have proven they will not stand for men attempting to push patriarchal agendas that undermine women's equality and expansion in corporate America. So, why are there so many white people involved in D&I? The answer: control, control, control because of fear, fear, and more fear!

Predominantly white administrations often use buzzwords like "tradition" and "history" to negate Black people and their impact on the nation's leading brands. From enslavement to consumerism, Black people have not benefited from traditions and history the way whites have. When corporate values are based on these hollow words, the takeaway for Blacks is that there is inherent, company-sanctioned bias within the corporation.

Note that even major brands are not major because they cater to all-white target markets; their customers are unique individuals from diverse backgrounds. Having an inclusive corporate environment enables companies to better understand their customer base and reflect it in their advertising and makeup to connect with their target markets. A considerable number of marketing studies have shown that positive images of any group draw that group toward a product based on the fact that they feel like it was made for them. In short, using positive imagery of a customer base is an acknowledgement that they "belong" and an invitation for them to engage. When consumers feel they can have a positive impact on a brand, they feel ownership, which leads to greater customer retention and brand loyalty. However, not depicting a group proactively nor revealing any form of leadership that matches the demographics of that specific market segment reflects the company sentiment of "we love your money, but we don't love you." The sentiments are presented in a more subliminal fashion, avoiding the direct statement of such appalling views. Yet, the sentiment is a small part of the ideological fight that leads to wearing down on both sides. Black executives also need to feel represented within a corporation or they become worn down, leading to less effective leadership and a waste of their inherent talent.

Making decisions that cannot be thwarted or revised by white traditionalists is possible and happens, but it doesn't happen often enough. Moreover, decisions made by Black executives pose great risks. If there is success as a result, the Black executive is celebrated by the majority of executives (except the hardcore traditionalists that might as well openly state they are racist or sexists). When Black executives make decisions that result in a loss, the Black executive faces even greater reprimand and punitive measures around than his or her white counterparts would in the same situation.

In horror movies, when the protagonist faces an unknown danger that lies just around the corner or in the dark, they often approach the unknown with ambiguous thoughts and actions, ready for fight or flight. The same goes for Black executives observing the unknown in real time. For instance, even when the results of Black leadership meet and exceed corporate expectations, if the means by which those results arose were not "traditional," the white traditionalists will continue their nonsensical attacks. Often, they will present "what if" arguments like "what if it didn't work out?" When a Black executive does succeed, they may minimize the victory by saying, "It had to be luck, and success is not based on luck… it's based on tradition." Again, consider the buzz word tradition and what it really means.

Consider the fact that many leading brands are not even 50 years old. So, why is there such a focus on so-called tradition when many companies such as IT firms don't have a history? The reason is racism and sexism didn't go away, they simply adapted to their environment like a virus adapting to a host who changed his or her diet, fitness regimen, or medication. The changing face of racism means that Black executives must train to fight against an unpredictable and shape-shifting opponent. Will they bob and weave, swarm the opponent to wear them down or rely on counter-punches to win the bout?

The greatest fear among executives is fear of the unknown. White people give each other the benefit of doubt that they don't give Black people, and the focus is never on the actual point Black people are making; rather, they focus on objectification and stereotype—the assumption that Black individuals are in some way "different" and that their views cannot be trusted. White traditionalist thoughts are not that original. They often follow along the lines of:

"Oh, Jamal [or Jamila] is only saying and doing this because he or she is Black—" [puts racial blindfolds on and earplugs in while staring at the Black executive]"He[she] is so angry. Obviously, his[her] point is rooted more in emotion than ethics or earnings... Uhhhh, how can I shut this show down and move onto something more important?"

By giving white people more leeway than Black people, corporations leave themselves open to make more mistakes that impact their brand's future for generations. Until white people stop allowing prejudicial thinking to take root and flourish within the corporate environment, talent will be lost, and valuable demographics will go untapped.

It's easy to point to problems in senior executive administrations or politicians marching about on the floors of Congress and scream, "Racism! Sexism!" and so many other negativeisms. Yet, when it comes to the very brands people of all colors invest in, the relationship between companies and their customers reflects the need for swallowing hard truths that white people need to face to remove the so-called traditionalists who maintain division.

Once division is attacked, the hierarchical system of corporations remaining loyal to histories and traditions that marginalize people of color, women of any color, and non-Christians, and the system of disenfranchisement itself will be disrupted by the self-enfranchisement among these various non-white (including non-male) groups. However, the focus on Black people, men and women, must be greater than on Latino, Native (Indigenous), or Asian people or white women. These groups have received a substantial amount of support for their ascension in corporate America, which has acted as a buffer to keep Black people (American, Caribbean, or African) out of positions of power for brands that would benefit from them most.

Blacks are up against a massive system of injustice, and the don't-hit-me punches they use to protect themselves are part of the silent agreement to maintain the status quo in exchange for the chance to climb in the ring. But Blacks are not the only ones who use this tactic against uncertainty and the powers that be. Republicans in the Senate and House made a silent agreement for five years once they bowed down and supported President Trump's ill-fated agenda. One of the most vocal examples was Senator Lindsey Graham. First, he stated Trump would be terrible for the party and the presidency.

Later, Graham defended Trump. Why? Trump was a powerful force in the party who could make or break a political career with a single tweet. Weak Republicans were in fear of him, but they were also concerned about upsetting constituents who may not have voted for Trump. Staying mostly silent while throwing the occasional don't-hit-me-punch made them look like they were taking their jobs seriously while they were really kowtowing to a want-to-be dictator.

After the insurrection, Graham famously whined, throwing his hands to the side on the floor of the Capitol, "I'm out! I'm out." He should have never bought into the madness. Much like Twitter, Facebook, Parler (later defunct), Fox and their silent agreements with Trump, Black executives pacify and placate white executives when they feel it is advantageous to do so. However, unlike the Republicans who were seduced into being Trumpublicans, the Black executive needs to look ahead and know—making a deal with or allowing the devil to run loose always ends terribly. The Black executive is like the pastor or priest trying to bind the devil. It's as if Black executives have to exorcise the racist demons of corporate America, but unlike the fearful boxer, the Black executive cannot rely on buying time in the fight by throwing don't-hit-me punches.

Black Republicans who served Trump present a good example of why Black executives shouldn't make deals with corporations. There was the irritating and tenacious Pastor Darrell Scott, the simple, happy-go-lucky Senator Tim Scott, the seemingly narcoleptic Secretary Ben Carson, and the late but great, Herman Cain and his business legacy, just to name a few. Unfortunately, Carson contracted COVID, possibly from exposure to non-mask-wearing Republicans and Trump flunkies. Herman Cain passed away from COVID in 2020. Trump never made any public attempt to honor either of these men. Regardless of what people think of them, they can learn from how making deals worked out for them.

The lesson these Black men leave us is that "if you can't beat them, join them" mentality doesn't fly in racist scenarios. Obviously, there's not enough time to discuss where these men went wrong. The focus is on what Black people with power, resources, and voices can do, not only to improve Black lives, but to continue to sustain our communities and work together with other Americans so that everybody wins. Yet, whether in politics, business, or even friendships, placing loyalty with people set on working against you is myopic—in short—it's stupid. Black executives can play the game long enough to gain footing and take action, but as Black people, they should never get too comfortable that they agree to be subjugated, denied, ignored, silenced, or sabotaged.

Black executives need to rope-a-dope or show a little footwork to avoid punches, stay clear of the corners, and buy some time until the bell rings, and they can regroup before getting back into the fight. Again, the fight is a matter of standing one's ground, staying loyal to one's values, inner constitution, and goals that meet the needs of African Americans or those for whom the Black executive fights. It's true that a Black executive should not feel pressured to be solely loyal to, or a representative of Black people, because this idea itself is racist. However, when it comes to Black issues and views, it is more strategic and sensible for corporations to seek a spectrum of Black executives, which means they need to have more than they can count on one hand among their various administrative teams.

"We're out of the excuses that have been used for a century to explain an acute under-representation of minorities in leadership positions," Pamela Newkirk, who included a chapter on the NFL in her book "Diversity Inc.: The Fight for Racial Equality in the Workplace," told me recently.

Hiring more Black executives—and getting out of their way to allow them to operate as leaders within the organization—will lead to cultures that truly celebrate diversity. Black and Brown employees and customers will recognize the difference. Putting a greater number of Black executives at the helm provides top-down modeling of how diversity can assist corporations to take a more inclusive approach to marketing to diverse customer bases by giving everyone a voice. It is not a matter of silencing the white traditionalist, rather, it's a matter of them relinquishing their views and getting on the same page with a multi-cultural, 21st-century America. Trumpism is a symptom of a diseased American culture and, like a mutation of COVID-19, it showed that this disease has the ability to mutate and become even more resistant to attempts to keep it in check. The only vaccine that will stop the spread of racism is a genuine commitment to stamping it out. When White executives realize that they are expected to listen to everyone and incorporate all views, there will be greater exchanges of ideas, perspectives, and values that will enhance and enrich the corporate culture. This will lead to better products and services, better revenues and profits, and substantial growth.

Once communication between various cultures is no longer a systemic issue, fewer don't-hit-me punches will be thrown, and everyone will be fighting to deliver their best. There are corporations that currently practice such pluralistic approaches to culture and leadership. However, until it is impossible to count such corporations on one hand, the vision of a multicultural, multifaceted corporate administration will remain out of reach.

One important thing for corporate leaders to understand is that Black executives are fighting for more than a seat at the table. They are fighting for the right to speak up for racial/cultural accuracy and authenticity while also asking to be seen as individuals who are unique for reasons other than their ethnicity. This can confuse traditionalists who want a Black and white way to define success. They may be bewildered by what D&I asks of them, thinking, "So, you want us to consult with you when there is a question about Black culture or customers, but you also want to be respected for being more than a Black man or woman."

When the root of centuries-old conflicts are explained like that, at face value it is confusing. But how many times do white men and women act upon racial/cultural perspectives under the guise of religious or political affiliation and, at the same time, state in various situations that they are an individual with thoughts and actions separate of so-called white culture? The ability to stand with our race, culture, gender, religion, and political affiliation without wearing that distinction like a yoke is what would make Black people equal to white people, whether that means not being pulled over for "driving while Black" or getting the promotions we deserve in C-suite positions.

Another key challenge that Black men and women face is that whites want to define us based on similarities and dissimilarities with white culture. For instance, the Christian Black executive is considered more approachable than the practicing Black Muslim or atheist. Of course, all white Americans are not Christian, but the majority are, and the belief that they are intrinsically more righteous because they are the majority is pervasive. Christianity is often used by whites to subjugate those of color, particularly people, and it gives white traditionalists a cloak behind which they can hide racist and racialized sexist perspectives and actions. They do not have to call it what it is. They simply call it Christianity (Dubrovensky, 2020).

Nevertheless, Black Christian men and women have an advantage in connecting with a predominantly Judeo-Christian leadership. But whites have learned to weaponize religion, too, using it to emotionally strong-arm Blacks into silent agreements. When a Black Christian executive does not agree with "business as usual" and rejects white traditionalist perspectives as false, manipulative, and dishonorable, the buzz phrase "Christian values" is used, and they face resistance, greater microaggressions, isolation, and eventual attacks to demote, transfer, or terminate the Black Christian executive (Dubrovensky, 2020).

This dynamic is especially effective at manipulating Black women, particularly Christian Black women. There is an untenable pressure for Christian Black women to be all things to all people—a perfect servant—which requires them to always perform above and beyond, as if they are superwomen. The expectations are higher for Black women because they have largely accepted this pressure to serve and overachieve, which makes them highly productive and less intimidating to white traditionalists. Black women are given more opportunities than Black men in corporate America, but loyalty is demanded, leading Black female executives to face feelings of isolation and untenable stress. If they fail to produce results that fall in line with the corporation, its mission, hierarchy, and system of values (presented as Christian values), they are shamed for failing to live up to the stereotype, essentially letting their culture down.

Pressing so-called Christian values on non-Christians is grounds for litigation for overt discrimination, but Black men and women are held to these manipulative standards due to the assumption that Black people will be agreeable to Christian values based on generations of socialization. This is why Muslim men and women who are African American are presented as novelties (positive employees) or outcomes of disagreeable diversity (negative) in White traditionalists' views (Dubrovensky, 2020).

The complexities of racism in the workplace make it easy for white traditionalists to pursue their agendas because the corporation wants to focus on business first. Racial conflict is seen as a distraction, and those who stir it up (i.e. Black men and women who are looking for equal treatment) are a hindrance to business as usual. In other words, the organization is so confident in its own right, it can easily dismiss don't-hit-me-punches as the flailing of a boxer who can't possibly win. Nevertheless, Black executives must be prepared to fight every day until a suitable environment with resources and opportunities are provided for all parties equally (Caldwell, 2017). They must fight to get white executives, who are quick to compartmentalize problems and deny adverse racial overtones in corporate America, see that Title VII of the 1964 Civil Rights Act is more than words on paper. It is a directive meant to correct covert and overt racism.

Of course, many white executives—like many whites—don't know they are racist. When they are in conflict with Black executives, they may believe the Black executive is working against tradition. Rather than face their own prejudices, they may simply say that a Black executive's ideas are too complex, too costly, or too radical. Finding business-based reasons to devalue Black work while claiming solidarity is racism with a smile, the remaining racist residue of knowing what's best for "Black folks" and believing one who is white is somehow better suited to lead because of their deep understanding of the core values of the given company. In that sense, Black executives constantly fight an uphill battle.

Even white women fighting for equality in the workplace have a better chance of victory simply because they share a vocabulary and worldview with the majority. The fact that white women are considered a minority is based solely on sexism, as they make up 36% of the total American population while white men make up 35%. white men often are quicker to support a white woman over others within corporate America due to a false sense of like-mindedness and their willing refutation of Black ideas. This act of controlling who gets in the ring even before the fight has begun is the result of systemic racism. Blacks are refused the right even to spar, because they are pre-labeled as overly sensitive, in search of conflict, and self-isolating based on their unwillingness to cooperate. The latter is a hold-over from the days of slavery when African Americans were coerced to perform through emotional and physical violence. Those who did not weren't seen as fighting for free will and equality—they were simply labeled uncooperative.

Collaboration is a hallmark of equality among groups of people. Through collaboration, both parties provide resources and receive equal benefits from the outcome. Unwillingness to cooperate in a corporate environment is the kiss of death, even when cooperating would mean submitting to a culture that works against, undermines, or disrespects Blacks. At face value, there is nothing wrong with trading blows for the sake of establishing and improving a brand. But when whites resort to microaggressions, racial stereotypes and dehumanizing behavior, it is no longer about business. Black executives must understand the rules of battle and refrain from throwing don't-hit-me punches to ward off low blows.

Another racist notion is that Blacks are only good workers when they are managed by a kind or giving white leader or supervisor. The so-called kindness is limited by how much Blacks are willing to "cooperate" and carry out the white leader's plan of operation. This transactional exchange kept many slaves alive long enough to eventually gain freedom. Most corporate leaders would not admit to the slightest hint of white patriarchal thoughts and actions in the workplace. Nevertheless, all-white C-suites represent exactly that—a board of white patriarchs lording over what they believe to be less capable laborers. To protect themselves from the need to acknowledge the imbalance, they shy away from any discussions of racial tension or conflict—especially when it is raised by Black executives. White executives often become infuriated by any insinuation that they are racist, yet, through their silence, they are able to quell racially motivated uprisings. There's no better way for white leaders to show true solidarity with the Black community than by listening to and validating the Black corporate experience, which will only happen when Blacks have a seat at the table.

Following the recent police shootings and protests that began in 2020, Corporate Social Responsibility (CSR) has become a buzzword for D&I initiatives. However, most corporations are just going through the motions without a deep commitment to change. Black executives can deliver a game-changing punch by holding these companies accountable for their stance. In other words, if Black executives stress the need for concrete results stemming from CSR, it will have a true impact on employees, executives, and corporate ethics.

For instance, until the Black Lives Matter riots, Quaker Oats had no issue with its 131-year run of Aunt Jemima products—even during the Obama years. Their recent choice to retire the brand and product line was reactive versus proactive, self-serving versus self-less. Their attempts at solidarity were less than solid. The company did what it did to capitalize on a movement, not to benefit Blacks. It is in situations like this that Black executives need to ball up their fists and continuously throw strong punches in the fight and let the opponents wear themselves out. Don't-hit-me punches tell the corporation that their meager attempts at solidarity are enough. They aren't. If Blacks really want to go for the knockout, they can join groups like Pull up for Change, a non-profit group that asks these companies to share the diversity and inclusion statistics within their own ranks—especially in leadership and C-suite roles. When they do, brands will no longer be able to get away with hiring for the optics, because they will know the question is coming: Does your stance line up with your stats?

When corporations embrace CSR on a deeper level than

shallow shows of solidarity and representation among market segments, Black executives will no longer have to pull any punches, because they will be empowered to fight with all they have. And while whites may worry that the fight they bring will be against traditionalism, the real fight is for the benefit of the corporation. Needed changes in leadership can and will lead to greater productivity and employee and customer retention, because when people feel valued by a brand, they are more willing to pay it back with loyalty, productivity, and profit.

Black executives must remember, they are fighting for more than just themselves as individuals. True, there were great battles in the 1940s following the Second World War, there were accomplishments made in the 1960s and 1970s, but honestly it is time for a reboot. When Blacks were allowed a glimpse of corporate inclusion in the1980s and 1990s, many Black people reconsidered their concept of Blackness. They were willing to trade their individual voices, experiences and cultures for corporate culture, because they believed it would pay off. They imagined themselves winning by knock-out, but what they found instead was intimidation and double-standards that required them to submit. To save face, they continued to throw don't-hit-me punches, believing they would be praised for their assertiveness. In fact, those weak punches left them feeling inauthentic and at the mercy of a system that can knock them out of the ring forever if they don't fall in line.

When they realized that corporate America would never let them fight in their own weight class, some of those men and women left to build strong, but smaller Black-owned companies. This represented a loss of talent to corporate America. The 2000s, even under President Obama, illustrated a downward slope in Black leadership. Recently, however, the push for Black leadership inside American businesses has returned to the forefront of education, political change, and social advocacy.

It is time for Black executives to realize that they have a legitimate opportunity to overturn tradition and land a fatal blow to white patriarchal and separatist notions currently accepted as the norm. But first, Black executives must be ready to relinquish the defensive strategy of don't-hit-me punches when they begin to tire of the fight. Now more than ever, perseverance and courage are required. Every Black executive should believe that they are clearing the way for more Black leaders to come after them, and they should punch with everything they have to get there.

WISDOM TO APPLY IN
THE CORPORATE RING:

• When white executives exhibit assertiveness—or even aggression—in the workplace, they are applauded as passionate, robust, and revolutionary. African Americans can have ideas that are all of these things, but they are read as threatening.

• Like these Black executives, some boxers become risk-averse, throwing punches only when they know they can score. They may put up great numbers, but you never really feel like they dominated. Instead of going for the knockout they leave it in the judges' hands. But fighting not to lose means one lacks the strategy, precision, and focus to win.

• Black executives that have allies and resources can curb the impact of white executives who pose opposition solely based on underlying racist notions of the American workforce established along classist, racist, and sexist lines.

• When White executives realize that they are expected to listen to everyone and incorporate all views, there will be greater exchanges of ideas, perspectives, and values that will enhance and enrich the corporate culture. This will lead to better products and services, better revenues and profits, and substantial growth.

- One important thing for corporate leaders to understand is that Black executives are fighting for more than a seat at the table. They are fighting for the right to speak up for racial/cultural accuracy and authenticity while also asking to be seen as individuals who are unique for reasons other than their ethnicity.

- Collaboration is a hallmark of equality among groups of people. Through collaboration, both parties provide resources and receive equal benefits from the outcome. Unwillingness to cooperate in a corporate environment is the kiss of death, even when cooperating would mean submitting to a culture that works against, undermines, or disrespects Blacks.

- Until white people stop allowing prejudicial thinking to take root and flourish within the corporate environment, talent will be lost, and valuable demographics will go untapped.

"

There is often less than total candor between Blacks and whites and the higher up you go the more that is true," says psychiatrist Price Cobbs. "There is mutual patronizing and misreading, making Blacks and whites unable to exchange ideas nd express their feelings.

"

BOXING STRATEGY

STAY ON THE INSIDE

When you don't have the same punching power as your opponent, squaring up against him or her can be a bad strategy. Instead, keep the fight on the inside for as long as you can by holding, hitting, and smothering. Essentially, you can wear down your opponent this way and win by amassing technical points.

ROUND 4

Ringside
SEATS

FOR those who live and breathe boxing, having ringside seats to a bout is a sign of prestige; it's how they can get as close to the fight as possible without actually being in the ring. For the Black professional in corporate America, ringside seats are like a glass ceiling—the point past which they will never be allowed to go, no matter how great their talents or how large their dreams of becoming a champion.

Boxers are sometimes given ringside seats when they aren't fighting. They are part of the experience, but they have little input and no power to show off their own abilities or expertise. It is much the same when corporate America allows Black executives to be near the action, but never controlling it. They are figureheads of inclusion.

In almost all industries, the middle management plateau strands African Americans in an observational position where they may feel seen and respected but are unable to test their skills at the highest levels and show what they are made of. Meanwhile, the path of true advancement is roped off, and they are forced to cheer on the mostly white, male executives who are allowed in the ring to compete.

When Black middle managers see their chances to compete literally sidelined, they make greater and greater sacrifices to prove themselves worthy. Over time, agitation builds as they see others reap the rewards that they are prevented from fighting for. They shadow box from their seats, imagining themselves landing knock-out after knockout when the reality is that their real fight is being on the wrong side of the ropes.

To be clear, it's no accident that Black men and women find themselves burdened with the managerial "privilege." These are the roles that white people are comfortable giving them because they are servile positions with limited power. Black leadership roles in corporate America can be hollow and exist solely to assist C-suite whites with what *they* deem important. In a sense, they become "pet" employees of predominantly white senior executive teams. Corporate America has a long history of casting Black employees as tokens or puppets that are charged with doing the actual work while whites sit back and use their "brains" to improve the bottom line. This good-ole-boy system ensures greater privilege, compensation, and respect is given to whites while it benefits from the myth that hard work pays off.

Unfortunately, Black executives have continued to submit and settle for secondary or auxiliary positions because those positions represent a way forward—what they may believe is a sound strategy for winning a seat at the decision-making table. The pressures of working while Black soon weigh them down, and with each successive rise, the barriers grow higher. Resistance to their growth can heighten the passion of Black professionals, making them harder and harder to keep down. Keeping them in a supportive role is a tactic that has been used by white people for centuries to underscore Black subservience and solidify the unwritten rules that help sustain Black suppression.

African Americans are no strangers to fighting from the side-lines for a seat at the table. In the 1950s and 1960s, African Americans were banned from eating at the same lunch counters as whites. This was true in cities and towns across the U.S. and especially in the South. In protest, sit-ins were organized by the N.A.A.C.P., Martin Luther King, Jr., and the Southern Christian Leadership Conference at Atlanta University. These sit-ins, in which young Black activists ignored the signs and took a seat, were a non-violent, civil-disobedience tactic that was met with harassment and humiliation at the hands of white citizens. Those who participated in sit-ins were prepared to be spat on, kicked, ignored by waitstaff, and generally intimidated.

The need for young men and women to prepare themselves for such harassment and violence did not end in diners. Six decades later, Blacks now fight for a seat at the corporate conference table, and we are elbowed, jostled, and shoved in our quest for workplace diversity. white leadership ignores, undermines, or disassembles efforts by Black men and women who have the skills, experience, and drive to succeed in executive and C-suite roles. Black executives no longer sit at the back of the bus; they can sit anywhere they want. But the opportunity to drive the bus, to determine the course of America's leading companies, continues to evade them.

While Black executives are no longer roped off from the balcony or mezzanine, they are roped off from participating in the main event. Some may see this as progress and believe they should be satisfied with the status quo, but others see it for what it is—continued subjugation from white leaders who refuse to cede or share power.

Young, Black executives must continue to move forward and never settle. The strategy of sitting until served is behind us. In corporate America, Blacks who simply wait for their turn can experience years of disappointment as promotions and raises pass them by. They may feel grateful to have a job and cling to the hope that one day their efforts will be recognized and rewarded, but corporate numbers don't lie. They have little hope of rising through the ranks without a fight.

In the 1950s and 1960s, some Blacks walked with King; others marched with Malcolm. Many later entered the Black Power Movement. Nevertheless, it took young, Black activists who were willing to undergo harassment to sit at lunch counter sit-ins or march down the streets despite the threats from angry whites. Sadly, the 2020s have underlined the importance of not becoming apathetic and compliant. Racism is still alive, and marches and protests are still necessary, even in the workplace. It's still alive because whites fear Blacks holding equal footing in the ring. They know that equality means they can no longer stand on the shoulders of Black men and women to make themselves look taller, so they must fight in their true weight class. Equality means they can no longer disqualify Blacks or keep them down by measuring against a separate scorecard. They know that equality means no more silent agreements.

The white Right backlash against President Obama demonstrates the profound fear whites have of African Americans taking power. There has never been a non-white group in America to claim, "We shall rule over the whites!" Yet white fear exists. It is guilt for the many ways they have held Blacks down for years. Guilt for either what many white people have done directly against people of color, specifically Black people, or the fact that whites benefit from their skin color alone. That guilt continues to fuel fears that the same inequities whites historically committed against Blacks shall come back upon them a hundredfold. Meanwhile, these same whites continue to uphold racism against Black people from Main Street to Wall Street by refusing them the right to compete as equals.

During early civil rights efforts, Black activists ignored

"Whites Only" signs and took their seats or joined freedom marches as a form of non-violent, civil disobedience. These non-violent protests were often met with violence from white mobs, cops, and K-9 units. In 2020, we witnessed more of the same from sadistic white cops who would unleash dogs, tear gas, rubber bullets, real bullets, and water hoses on protesting African Americans marching for freedom from police brutality. The difference is today's fight has changed. Black protesters are no longer willing to bring bullhorns to gunfights. Today's Black protesters take precautions against the tear gas and violence, standing ready to defend themselves against the fascist forces of American law enforcement, which are set on attacking peaceful Americans exercising their First Amendment rights.

Black executives can learn about preparation from these brave Americans. Rather than walking forward with caution to avoid being the target of workplace racism, they can expect it, and must respond as if they had been attacked, because they have. This perspective is not hostile, but just and proactive. Black freedom fighters can no longer sit silently and accept the abuse. A more assertive and aggressive march in which things aren't so easy for the racists and fascists is in demand. Whether in the streets, in our school rooms, our courtrooms or in the board rooms of corporate America, Black people are coming together as an immutable, unyielding force that recognizes its own God-given power and exercises it accordingly. The fight for a voice in the C-suites of America companies may not be as high profile as the demonstrations we now see in the streets, but it is every bit as vital. Black executives must stop thinking about self-preservation alone and understand that when they settle for ringside seats to the fight, they are giving up their chance at the championship and ultimately making it harder for other African Americans to take their place in the ring as well.

A history of slavery and subjugation has taught African Americans to focus on survival and being strong enough to continue regardless of loss: loss of freedom, loss of history, loss of culture, and even loss of family in years past when men and women were traded like cattle. To make true progress toward equality, young Black fighters must now look beyond survival and recoup past losses by coming out strong, stalwart, and steadfast. The problem is, they don't have many examples of people who look like them dominating in the ring, and they haven't had the endurance training it will take to leave the ring victorious.

What good is endurance to a runner who cannot conceive of a finish line? What good is endurance to a boxer who is never evenly matched and must fight opponent after opponent, regardless of the outcome? It's time Blacks realized that the game played in corporate America is based on working smarter not harder. Black men and women will never triumph by enduring years on the wrong side of the ropes. They cannot attain C-level positions by working harder than their white peers, because being the workhorse only makes them valuable as workhorses. Instead, Black executives must not get lost in their work and lose sight of the rewards within striking distance. Just like their ancestors sang generations ago, it's time to "Keep your eyes on the prize." Rather than submitting to a fixed fight, it is time that Black executives call out the injustice and refuse to be roped off from the action.

While this may sound daunting, African Americans are forced to operate in battle mode for most of their lives, and they are more prepared than they think. What currently holds us back is exhaustion. We are tired of fighting for basic rights like fair housing, access to healthcare, and the means to pursue an education. The school-to-jail pipeline must be replaced by a school-to-skill pipeline that ensures they have mentors and advocates along the way. Today, Black students who fight hard to graduate, who avoid the millions of pitfalls between where they came from and where they want to go, fall between the cracks and work jobs that stifle or ignore their executive potential just to fight another day. Young, Black professionals need a clear path for moving beyond management and supervisory positions in major corporations. True, there are Black networking organizations that students can join, but training under someone who has never been allowed in the ring either isn't enough. Corporations should be creating space for Blacks at the corporate table as an invitation. White leaders who want to make a difference should place empty chairs in the boardroom and vow to fill them with the best and brightest Black candidates they can find. When they say they can't find qualified Black candidates, they need look no further than the ringside seats.

The systematic sidelining of Black talent is endemic to American culture, and it is not difficult to find brilliant African Americans wasting their talents in toxic environments. Emory University offers one such example. Like many other scholastic and research institutions, its leaders have failed to acknowledge racist practices that sideline African American staff members. Nathan McCall, former Emory faculty member and author of *Makes Me Wanna Holler*, notes the ways in which the university abuses and neglects African American faculty, negating their professional, educational, and financial progress. When Black staff members bring challenges or problems they were facing to the administration, they were often ignored, pacified, or threatened with losing their position, and with the position, the prestige of working at Emory University. In 2020, the fallout from racial and civil unrest related to white supremacy and police violence, University President Gregory L. Fenves, started a campaign to address racism and increase D&I awareness. As part of this effort, Emory has begun to review its policing policies, which have led to unwarranted arrests and harassment of students of color. The fact that an institution of higher learning must review their own role in the school-to-jail pipeline may be shocking to some, but to Black men and women, it is simply a symptom of the systematic racism they have faced their whole lives.

This system, which is baked into the foundation of American education, politics, economics, and social culture, puts undo emphasis on race to alert those at the top of the power structure to pos-sible insurrection. Historically, the people at the top happen to be predominantly white men and women—especially in the American South. Through their own unwillingness to embrace Americans of different racial and cultural perspectives, they propagate the abuse of Black students and would-be professionals in conscious and unconscious ways to keep them from infiltrating the upper echelons of society. Whether Black people conform or rebel, they are distracted by fighting the system again and again just to survive, which makes it harder for them to focus on their own educational and professional agenda. In boxing terms, this is a feint—a move that causes no noticeable damage to the opponent, but effectively distracts them. Feints are designed to convince an opponent you're about to do one thing before they realize you've switched it up with another punch aimed at a different spot. Feints allow corporations to predict what their Black executives will do, thus allowing them to stay in the dominant position.

Blacks have found that publicly calling out racism when they see it is one of the best defenses. Nothing matters more to American corporations than money, and money comes from customers of all backgrounds, races and genders. Calling out the lack of diversity in the C-suites of America is one way to avoid distraction techniques and hit them where it hurts.

Corporate brands secretly fear the loss of historically invested white clientele who may or may not take proactive interest in whether a company embraces diversity and inclusion. It becomes a financial question: is racism more profitable than diversity? We have yet to see, but certainly part of the answer lies in the power of Black executives to call out inequality when they see it and let the public decide.

Meanwhile, Black professionals are still being left out. For instance, they are forced to sit ringside on occasions of white, workplace camaraderie, including lunches, private meetings, happy hours and late night get togethers. African Americans of various levels within a corporation are often also threatened by so-called budget cuts to their departments as if they are auxiliary, never mainstream. Those threatened are often leaders of the Race Relations or Diversity and Inclusion departments of corporations. The scenario is the same, it places Black professionals in positions where they don't want to make too many waves for fear of being replaced or not having the significant permanency or tenure. Black professionals understand they need permanency and tenure in order to be treated with the respect given to white staff members of equal ranking, education, and experience.

All of these scenarios (with which white executives need not grapple) slow Black professionals and executives down, even when they would otherwise excel. This leads many Black men and women to forfeit their professional journey, which is a loss to the corporate world. Black employees represent Black interests, the interests of other people of color, and means for the company to connect with diverse people and drive profits. When Black people walk away from corporate culture, it is America that loses.

On the flip side, those Black professionals that do stay often make silent agreements not to rock the boat, which perpetuates the behavior that drives out key talent in the first place. As a reward, African Americans are selected as members of a team or assistants, rarely as the first-string of lead senior executives (McCall, 2020).

As with boxing, THE STATS ARE WHAT MATTER HERE:

Nearly 70% of African American applicants proved more qualified than white male counterparts, and yet, they continue to struggle in their efforts to rise through the ranks (Bush, 2020; Beckwith, Carter, & Peters, 2016). Black women have had a particularly hard time gaining leadership positions, even as they continue to make gains in education.

◀⭐▶ By 1980, Women outnumbered men on college campuses and earned 33% of law degrees. By 2002, women earned more undergraduate business degrees than men and made up 50% of candidates entering firms for key positions. Yet by 2010, there were only 15 female Fortune 500 CEOs, only one was Black, Ursula Burns of Xerox. (Beckwith, Carter, & Peters, 2016).

◀⭐▶ Today, women of color only represent 1.1% of corporate officers (assistant senior executives and board members) in Fortune 500 companies. Women in general hold 11.9% of managerial and professional positions, but African American women make up a mere 5.3%. Following 2017, when Rosalind Brewer the CEO of Sam's Club resigned, there were no longer any African American women of national or global C-suite status within a Fortune 500 company.

◀⭐▶ The journey of all Black executives is rife with imaginary obstacles, but Black women in particular are in danger of being stereotyped by white men. For instance, when African American women assert themselves, they are often seen as aggressive, which is a trait that helps men but can hurt women. Conforming to sexist norms by "toning it down" is the equivalent of making a Silent Agreement in exchange for ringside seats.

◄✪► For Black women to be successful in corporate America, they must collaborate but not conform. Many Black women join networks that enable them to get around the good-ole-boy system, but the underlying problem persist: Corporations function from the perspective of the dominant culture, which is white and male. White women have an easier time adjusting to a corporate environment because they share cultural ties with white men (Beckwith, Carter, & Peters, 2016, p. 117).

◄✪► One remedy for Black women, and African Americans in general, is to seek out mentorships for themselves. Mentorships can help prepare them for senior executive positions and the cultural expectations that come with them. Corporations should be putting such programs in place to support the growth of African Americans, and Black women in particular. Women make up 50% of the world's working population but only establish 37% of the Gross Domestic Product, which points to underrepresentation that demands greater investment into the female and female of color workforce (Babarinsa, 2020, p. 12).

It has been noted that three areas of focus should be considered when implementing diversity management interventions within a corporation: affinity groups, mentoring, and training and development initiatives (Bush, 2020; Beckwith, Carter, & Peters, 2016). Six primary factors both enrich and enhance career development and potential for Black executives. These six factors include possessing a doctoral degree, being recognized as a national organization member, having collaborative and consolidating communication skills, being supportive of other people, having administrative and executive experience, and being mobile, nationally and internationally. Unfortunately, many Black men and women employ the aforementioned strategies and still find that their mediocre white colleagues are selected for C-suite positions by white senior executives.

◄✪► Negative outcomes can arise only when a Black professional doesn't know how to make the most of support or leverage opposition. It has been shown that opposition can drive more support for certain ideas or policy changes. Confidently facing and overcoming opposition shows leadership and builds a case for senior executive positions. The key is to know people who can get things done, either by providing services, goods, or processes. The more gatekeepers with which candidates establish balanced relationships, the more access to various paths, resources, opportunity, exposure, and leadership one possesses (Bush, 2020; Beckwith, Carter, & Peters, 2016).

◄✪► Finding support for mentorship and feedback, seeking to be on committees or internships, seeking experience that displays talent, and maintaining work-life balance are primary strategies in establishing oneself as a primary candidate for senior level positions. However, for many African Americans, it's also a matter of generating opportunity. For some, this means traveling abroad to gain work experience.

◖✪◗ According to the Executive Leadership Council's Institute for Leadership Development & Research, key strategies to use when ascending the corporate ladder include maintaining longevity in one position, team, or department in a leading supervisory role, and making sure all accomplishments are noted by the CEO and other C-suite members of the company. Maintaining any form of mentorship (even with mentors that are demographically different) establishes a portfolio of experiences for senior executives to review. Maintaining relationships that are strong and always in a process of exchange and productivity show a candidate is calm, organized, and able to lead within administration (Coachman, 2009).

◖✪◗ Corporations in these trying social, political, and economic times often try to practice "color blindness," but there is more demand for "color embrace." Diversity and Inclusion departments need direct, accessible, and transparent C-suite support. White men should head some diversity-based assignments for the sake of involvement. Black employees should assess the effectiveness of D&I endeavors every year with a primary focus on mitigating racism and racialized sexism and generating greater plurality and diversity support.

◖✪◗ To truly avoid bias and assumptions, corporations must walk away from a one-size fits all approach to diversity and replace it with culturally relevant solutions. Mentoring opportunities should not be used to encourage African Americans to compromise personal beliefs and values simply to conform. Embracing full diversity for its own sake has proven effective. Leading global management consulting firm McKinsey & Company found that when companies incorporate racial and gender-based diversity, they outperformed other less diverse companies, specifically those with predominantly white male leadership.

◖✪◗ Companies are created to provide products, processes, or services to customers to generate a profit. When a business expands into new market segments, the business must incorporate the segment fully to build solid relationships with customers. They not only make purchases, but they become return customers who provide residual income, making them de facto investors in the future of the business. Yet, even when corporations recognize the need to connect with new and untapped demographics like Black Americans, they often fail to promote the very people who might be seen as representative of that market segment. white leaders may give African American executives ringside seats for the optics, but when they sit down to make decisions, they return to their white echo-chamber of ideas.

⬛⭐⬛ Conscious companies and organizations working with authentic Black leadership understand the value of organizational learning implemented through diversity and inclusion initiatives. These initiatives increase job satisfaction, reduce turnover rates, assist in leadership development, and enhance the adaptability of American businesses to be more inclusive and interconnected with their various networks of stakeholders (employees, customers, the national and global community) (Valamis, 2020).

⬛⭐⬛ It is unwise to include Black faces on executive teams for show if they are pressured to promote white perspectives, perspectives which ignore, negate, or distort Black images, values, or concerns. This is not a sign of progressive thinking. Consumers are loyal to brands that represent them, plain and simple. The best way to represent consumers is by investing in leadership that shares the same convictions, history, and experiences as the consumers (Taha, 2020). Nonetheless, as consumers and as professionals within corporate America, there is a need for bridging sociopolitical, ethical, and culturally relative exchanges between the social and the corporate sector, between businesses and their consumers within their everyday lives. It's time to put cultural messaging and ownership back into the hands of Black leaders, Black innovators, Black artists, Black influencers, Black photographers, and Black storytellers.

◄✪► Unfortunately, just 10% of U.S. businesses are owned by Black men and women. This is not a coincidence. It is the result of an age-old, hierarchal system of disenfranchisement and subjugation designed to maintain a white male power structure over a diverse, pluralistic society (Roberts & Mayo, 2019).

◄✪► When corporations exclude Black men and women from entering the corporate ring, a single demographic, white males, sets the tone for recruiting, hiring, promoting, developing, and then following the lead of executives who are ethically, socio-politically, and economically responsible for the growth and expansion of American business (Roberts & Mayo, 2019)

◄✪► A 2015 McKinsey & Company report notes that among the top 25% of 366 public companies, those that supported ethnic and racial diversity in leadership and administration possessed a 35% advantage to gain financial returns superior to the industry mean versus those companies who did not provide equal support. Yet, despite the focus on diversity training and ethics, African American progress toward top management roles remains slow to nonexistent, partially because Black leaders trade professional progress for a ringside seat.

◄✪► It's time Black executives recognize that ringside seats are not an honor but an impediment to true progress. Rather than train for a seat on the sidelines of corporate America, they must demand their chance in the ring. Often, they need better promoters to do this. Talented, professional boxers have seen their careers hobbled by promoters who are more invested in other fighters and fail to get them the fights they need to prove their worth. The same is true for African American executives. No matter how talented they are, every Black executive needs a strong promoter (i.e. mentor) who will not only get them into the ring but ensure that they are evenly matched and positioned for victory. Corporations that are committed to diversity will match promoters with fighters to ensure that the talent they have invested in continues to grow and thrive. Every employee is a potential heavyweight champion, but without the proper training and promotion, white employees will continue to dominate the ring at the expense of the corporation itself.

WISDOM TO APPLY IN
THE CORPORATE RING:

- In almost all industries, the middle management plateau strands African Americans in an observational position where they may feel seen and respected but are unable to test their skills at the highest levels and show what they are made of. Meanwhile, the path of true advancement is roped off, and they are forced to cheer on the mostly white, male executives who are allowed in the ring to compete.

- Black men and women will never triumph by enduring years on the wrong side of the ropes. They cannot attain C-level positions by working harder than their white peers, because being the workhorse only makes them valuable as workhorses.

- Historically, the people at the top happen to be predominantly white men and women—especially in the American South. Through their own unwillingness to embrace Americans of different racial and cultural perspectives, they propagate the abuse of Black students and would-be professionals in conscious and unconscious ways to keep them from infiltrating the upper echelons of society.

• Corporate brands secretly fear the loss of historically invested white clientele who may or may not take proactive interest in whether a company embraces diversity and inclusion. It becomes a financial question: is racism more profitable than diversity?

• To truly avoid bias and assumptions, corporations must walk away from a one-size fits all approach to diversity and replace it with culturally relevant solutions. Mentoring opportunities should not be used to encourage African Americans to compromise personal beliefs and values simply to conform.

• Conscious companies and organizations working with authentic Black leadership understand the value of organizational learning implemented through diversity and inclusion initiatives. These initiatives increase job satisfaction, reduce turnover rates, assist in leadership development, and enhance the adaptability of American businesses to be more inclusive and interconnected with their various networks of stakeholders (employees, customers, the national and global community) (Valamis, 2020).

"

Blacks
have found that
publicly calling out
racism when they
see it is one of the
best defenses.

"

BOXING STRATEGY

PUSH FORWARD

When opponents are in a higher weight class, you must use their strength against them or use techniques to wear them down. When pushing forward, you tie up your opponent's arms and push back at the same time, using up their energy to buy yourself time. Once you've pushed your opponent into a corner or onto the ropes and worn them out, you have more freedom to land multiple punches.

Punching Above Your
WEIGHT CLASS

IN the boxing world, athletes compete by weight class, ensuring a reasonably fair fight. In the corporate world, executives largely compete based on superficial stereotypes that—even in 2021—still elevate white male superiority and entitlement above all else. Fairness rarely enters the ring. Obviously, this makes it harder for women and non-white races to compete, and among this subgroup of employees, there is also a pecking order in which Black men and women rank last. As a result, African American executives must always punch above their weight class just for the opportunity to compete.

A study conducted by Korn Ferry found that Black corporate

leaders are some of the highest performing. This is because they have to be to survive in corporate America. According to the study, nearly 60% of Black P&L leaders report having to work twice as hard and accomplish twice as much as their peers to counter misperceptions about their skills and results. More than 35% said they were assigned extremely tough projects that had a high risk of failure because there was an expectation that they needed to prove themselves.

Meanwhile, the punches Black executives take over and over again can become soul-crushing. It is not just a challenge for Black men and women to move up the corporate ladder or be invited into the C-suite hierarchy, it is a championship fight that only the toughest, most passionate, and most focused can win.

Training for this fight starts early on in most Black careers—sometimes even before a Black men or women is first hired. African Americans are turned away time and time again for having "Black sounding names," and they are intimidated in interviews by the white gaze. One study showed that by "whitening" their resumes (i.e. removing racial cues like black-sounding names), 25% of black candidates received callbacks while only 10% got calls when they left ethnic details intact. it isn't much better once they are hired. Questions, concerns, and doubts shape the decisions of young, Black executives as they bob and weave against an uncertain, but certainly powerful opponent.

Furthering their education is one of their first jabs many African Americans take at gaining traction in the corporate world, yet even those with Master's degrees face competition from whites with no more than Bachelor's or high school diplomas. This misalignment of competing candidates perpetuates the marginalization of Black candidates. Corporations repeatedly prove that they hire and promote along racial lines with every white face in their boardrooms, and every brown or black face that is absent.

Blacks who choose to pursue further education or participate in tuition reimbursement programs to be promotion-worthy often find they don't have the time, money, or confidence in themselves or the value of their degrees, knowing that their efforts may not be recognized. When job-furthering educational needs can't be met due to these limitations, African American professionals sacrifice future fights because they are already fighting above their weight class, and they still can't get ahead. This cycle of impaired career growth is rarely recognized or remedied by corporations that rely on white networking to fill their C-suites. There are always those who will claim that institutional racism doesn't exist and that the corporate structure is based on merit alone, but the fact is that African Americans make up roughly 13% of the American population, yet only about 1% of board members in the S&P 500 and less than 1% of CEOs are Black, and only 3 African American women have led Fortune 500 companies. (SHRM, 2021)

It's no wonder that nearly one in five Black professionals feel that someone of their race or ethnicity would never achieve a top position at their company. White executives have long benefited because people of color have less access to high-quality education and high-wage employment and are often forced into low-paying commercial and household jobs, from coal mining and call-center work to cleaning, cooking, and caregiving. To climb the steep hill to the C-suite, African American men and women have to work harder than their white counterparts to prove that they are more than capable, that they are "part of the team," and that they are willing to blend into the dominant culture, which is often very different than their own.

Disenfranchisement and social racism go hand in hand. Blacks are also afforded fewer loans and credit-based supports that would enable them to compete with whites. They are much less likely to have inherited generational wealth because of past restrictions that limited their family's ability to build assets.

The stereotypes that haunt Blacks also subject them to greater scrutiny, starting when they are young. Minor childhood mistakes, such as wearing a hoodie in a store, can result in jail time that leaves marks on their records and reaffirms stereotypes about Black youth. Some of the harshest disciplinary actions are exhibited white staffs at predominantly Black schools. Such disciplinary actions later repeat themselves in the legal system in the form of racial profiling, false arrests, police brutality, police shootings, severe legal judgments, and overrepresented incarceration rates, establishing a school-to-jail pipeline that ensnares many Black children and youth. This pervasive system of vilifying Black children and ferrying them into the legal system makes those Blacks who successfully enter the corporate world seem suspect. What was their background? How did they come to be here, and what of the world they come from did they bring with them?

The Black professional faces other types of racism that extend beyond these blatant forms. American society remains fixated on a Eurocentric perspective that shapes the system in which other racial and cultural norms are perceived or defined as being valuable or not. This perspective determines how certain people are perceived, presented in media, politics, or spoken of when none of that demographic are present in the conversation. This is the invisible opponent that African American professionals battle when they are punching above their weight class.

When African Americans conquer yet another obstacle of institutional racism, often the powers-that-be invent new rules that still result in disqualification. Because of this and a million other subtle and not-so-subtle ways that America pushes Blacks down when they try to rise, young Black people spend more time training for survival than training for success. Whites have a vested interest in preventing Blacks from gaining power, because Blacks may use that power to make the fight fair, displacing those who feel superior based on the color of their skin alone.

A wide range of American people who immigrated from places like the Caribbean or Europe are considered "Black" because of their skin tone, but in corporate America, all of them are tagged with the African American label. I blur this distinction throughout this book due to the complex undercurrents of societal meaning mixed with individual layers of racial identity. "African American" is the accepted, politically correct way to refer to dark-skinned people in America, but it is technically inaccurate in many cases. Tagging every Black person as African American is convenient for whites who mentally draw a direct line from dark skin to slavery and from slavery to economic struggle and disadvantage and from disadvantage to a lack of skills and sophistication.

Influential Black men and women such as Crispus Attucks, Phyllis Wheatley, Paul Cuffe, Prince Hall, Elijah McCoy, Frederick Douglas, Ida B. Wells, Marcus Garvey, W.E.B. DuBois, Booker T. Washington, A. Phillip Randolph, to Dr. King, Malcolm X, Shirley Chisolm, President Barack Obama and even the current Vice President, Kamala Harris are seen as exceptions to the rule that dark-skinned people are less than, yet many whites paint them with the same, racist brush thereby erasing their rich lineages and defining how they should be viewed. If ever corporate America were to stop forcing all dark-skinned people into this system of negative stereotyping, Blacks of all origins might have a better chance to compete based solely on merit and not on an imagined world-view, but that day is far away.

Being defined in Eurocentric terms limits the potential of dark-skinned Americans to rise in the ranks of corporate America, because corporations still believe white mediocrity to be superior to Black excellence. To validate this point of view, corporations continuously raise the bar to undermine Black economic, occupational, and financial progress. It is not a matter of intelligence, experience, or skillset. Instead, the professional placement of African Americans is based on the predominantly white administration's whims and personal stereotypes of Black individuals. Too often, Black professionals are spoken of as difficult, not team players, boastful, or merely the product of affirmative action. The hard work and accomplishments of Blacks are dismissed as luck or offset by perceived personality defects.

Black professionals can begin to feel that dealing with racism is just part of their job. Any mention of the fact that they are outmatched by corporate bigotry feeds into the stereotype that African Americans are complainers who want to get ahead without their dues. Ironically, these criticisms usually come from white people who paid their dues by being white.

One of the most effective ways for Blacks to continue to punch above their weight class is to use their opponents' strengths against them. Whites by far have the greatest share of voice in

American corporate leadership, so forcing them to voice their commitment—or lack of commitment—to diversity is a start. Many Black professionals are banding together with third-party allies to monitor which companies are hiring African Americans for advanced positions, specifically companies that claim they support Black promotion and progress. One such example is the group "Pull up for change," which has taken Instagram by storm and is asking these companies to "pull up or shut up" by sharing the diversity and inclusion statistics within their own ranks—especially in leadership and C-suite roles.

Sharon Chuter, CMO of **UOMA Beauty,** created the non-profit to hold major corporations accountable for their roles in the systemic oppression of African Americans. She says, "We spend money, we don't own anything, nobody employs us. So, we continue to spend money, but nobody gives us that money back."

To remedy this imbalance, Chuter is pushing major companies to acknowledge it for themselves in hopes of creating change. Those brands that aren't willing to do so face a backlash in the form of further scrutiny and boycotts as more Black men and women start to vote with their wallets.

This approach puts the onus back on white leaders. UC Santa

Cruz research professor in social psychology, Tom Pettigrew says, "Most of the time stereotypes are mere shadow images rooted in one's history and deep in the subconscious. While blatant bigotry is a problem in organizations, neutrality may be an even greater obstacle to Blacks. While an estimated 15% of white Americans are extremely antiblack, 60% are more or less neutral and conform to socially approved behavior."

Whether it is apathy or conscious racism, calling it out essentially requires corporations to defend their stance. When this happens, the weight class shifts and the fight becomes fairer. Measuring actual statistics against empty promises forces corporate leaders to examine their hiring practices and whether they are selecting staff based on merit, experience, and work ethic or race and stereotypes alone. Calling out the numbers of Blacks in leadership positions moves the conversation from one about an individual's merits in a rigged fight to one of equitable rules. Imagine if the American Boxing Federation decreed that Blacks could only participate as featherweight fighters and whites were all heavyweight champions. Now imagine that those featherweights had to beat a heavyweight in order to be in the ring at all. Boxing would quickly deteriorate into a farce in which race meant more than skill or talent.

That is exactly what's happening in corporate boardrooms across America.

Even on the occasions that a Black executive is allowed to fight at his or her level of expertise, it may still be for the optics and the fight is still fixed in favor of the remaining majority of whites. Black professionals are not looking to be token space fillers in corporations; rather, they demand to be recognized and imbued with the authority to lead as they deserve, to lead American corporations as fully incorporated Americans.

If corporations really wanted to shift this dynamic, they would see help from Black thought leaders—the very people they claim to support in the fight against inequality. Enough is enough. It's time to hire people who can enrich American companies the top down versus allowing them to burn themselves out from the bottom up fighting a system they can't beat.

To enact real change, white corporate leaders must admit the problem is rooted in personal selections and skewed hiring practices. They must make a personal and professional investment in fostering diversity in order to see substantial growth. And they must stop requiring Black candidates to perform above their weight classes simply for a chance to compete.

Due to historical disenfranchisement, specifically in corporate America, African American employees often experience anxiety when potential conflict with their Caucasian co-workers arises. This apprehension can undermine their willingness to participate in social versus professional interactions that can make or break a career. Eventually, the sense of isolation and fear over potential mistakes leads to many Black employees—from entry-level to executives—to leave their companies and accept non-administrative, race-based executive positions. They may strive only to remain in the same positions for as long as possible or accept being bounced around as a space-filler or guinea pig for race-related projects. There has to be a wider path to C-suite positions.

Those Black executives who remain often suffer from a sense of fatigue over time. The fatigue is rooted in feeling ingenuine because they are a different person with family and friends than they are at work where speaking their minds can cause coworkers to question their loyalty to white authority or their authenticity as Blacks. Some say it's not a matter of race or culture; certain behaviors, like laughing too loud, are just inappropriate. At times, everybody, male or female, Black or white, spontaneously laughs when surprised, excited or happy. Yet completely natural reactions like this can be politically charged for African Americans who are continually measured by white attitudes, perspectives, and codes of conduct.

Blacks are sometimes seen as too emotive or boisterous when they do exactly what whites do. Not knowing when being human will become a deficit to them, many Blacks practice code switching or changing their personality to fit in. By over compensating in this way, Black professionals lose themselves to merely appease the dominant white culture.

With little support, many African American professionals built their foundations for success not on achievement alone but on grappling with how they appear to others. No matter what choices African American professionals make, they make them with focus on the worst-case scenario which erodes their ability to fully and truthfully add to certain discussions or decisions. When this subtle form of suppression goes unchecked, corporations lose out on the full potential of their hires and miss opportunities to benefit from a unique point of view.

Regrettably, corporations retain an antiquated mindset that harkens back to slavery. The main tenet of this mindset is that white people should be in a position to "work" Black people rather than work with or for them. This is why Black talent is over-represented in the lower strata of American corporations (think warehouse workers or janitors) and underrepresented in higher executive positions based on erroneous, antiquated notions of undereducated, overly expressive Blacks only being fit only to serve under the steady hand of the superior white patriarchy. In this belief system, the white patriarchy is like a parent that knows what is best for Blacks. Again, this maintains the imbalance of power that benefits whites in the workplace. Blacks must learn to punch above their weight class just to be taken seriously.

But punching above their weight class has had a surprising effect on Black labor fighters. Working twice as hard to receive half as much has made tasks that are in their weight class seem simple. Like an outmatched boxer, Black executives begin to look at the long game and become savvy technical fighters. When every successful swing is on paper, they can eventually—as long as they don't get knocked out—compile enough evidence to prove their worth to the judges or white C-suite leadership. Unfortunately, there are too many other forces at work to turn this approach into a victory, and many Blacks who have tired of the fight decide it is time to use their talents for themselves by opening Black businesses.

When Black professionals are free agents on the open market, they, unsurprisingly, do very well because they have honed their skills to perfection by always punching up. While almost every businesses suffered during the COVID-19 pandemic, Blacks may have been more psychologically prepared to pivot because most never feel they have job security to begin with. The concurrent racial strife that swept the United States in response to the Black deaths at the hands of the police resulted in the pandemic-proof Black Lives Matter movement because of the internal drive Blacks possess. Despite the obvious danger to their health, Black protesters took up the mantle of justice and fought hard to keep the focus on getting a fair fight.

Black entrepreneurs have benefitted greatly from this movement, with many Black business owners experiencing an uptick in new customers that come from various backgrounds within the African Diaspora (i.e. Caribbean Americans, American Africans, Afro-Latinos, and Afro-Europeans). These business leaders didn't do it with much help. From 2007 to 2017, over 50% of Black-owned companies were denied for loans. The denial rate for white business owners was only 25%. Despite this financial disadvantage, Black market share has increased and African American business leaders have made it clear that if they can't compete in a fair fight in eurocentric corporate America, they can successfully compete in the marketplace where the majority of citizens are considered a minority.

2020 marked the year in which June 19th or Juneteenth became a recognized federal holiday. On that day in 1865, the last enslaved Black people in America were emancipated. The celebration of Juneteenth is a celebration of freedom. Having that day recognize by corporate America is a small signal that the tides may be shifting, and even staunchly conservative, white leaders realize that to serve a diverse customer base they must embrace diversity within their corporate structure.

The more diverse American society becomes, the more companies that incorporate diversity into their business models will thrive. Recently, Proctor & Gamble (P&G) Chief Brand Officer, Mark Pritchard, stated that there is a need for the creative supply chain (i.e. brands, agencies, and production crews) to reflect the spectrum of target markets, specifically people of color, and he announced P&Gs commitment to multicultural representation. Pritchard stated that P&G would substantially invest more in Black-owned-or-operated media companies, agencies, and marketing suppliers, not based on economic necessity or financial gain alone but to change the very culture of corporate America and consciously incorporate African Americans. In that sense, as boxers, African Americans could up their weight class as far as battling in the ring among other candidates for C-suite positions removing historical disenfranchisement to some degree. Not only is P&G changing its approach and assessment of hiring more African Americans for key positions, but also portraying African Americans in an accurate and respectful manner (WARC, 2020).

Still, the input of African American leaders inside of American corporations is still token and insignificant in comparison to the decision-making powers of white corporate executives. But as the racial makeup of America continues to diversify, these old guard companies will find it difficult to compete as non-white consumers continue to vote with their dollars. The result may well be that weight classes will no longer be defined by white men, but by consumers themselves.

In an effort to keep up with the changing times, some corporations have used deceptive practices to blend demographics and boost diversity numbers while overshadowing the underlying lack of true diversity and inclusion of people of color within their four walls. Various companies present their statistics for white women to represent the entire non-white male population. White women are a diverse demographic, ethnically, religiously, and in terms of sexual orientation, but they are still a majority of the population compared to white men. This type of number-juggling serves to further obfuscate the lack of true diversity throughout all industries. Such misleading statistics drive a growing number of young, ambitious, and entrepreneurial Black executives to leave corporate America, feeling yet another bar has been raised.

Black professionals understand that there is a system, an institution of racial barriers that permeate all major corporations, even the newest and most innovative areas such as IT. Therefore, they attempt to conform with the hope that racism will not create conflict or that they can appear non-threatening enough to be promoted while punching hard enough to stay in the fight. When Black professionals are forced into a double-consciousness in which they become someone else to conform to corporate norms, they can lose balance and find themselves moving from company to company, from position to position, in an effort to find a fit. To corporate leadership, this behavior appears inconsistent, and Blacks are again penalized for their lack of direction or focus. Black professionals know they are being cheated, but they are unable to balance the scales because they are fighting from a position of weakness.

The basis of this knotty problem lies with white C-suite executives who ignore the obvious inequalities or use deflection and denial to avoid addressing it. The White executive who reads an account of a Black professionals being denied promotions and opportunities may think, "I'm sure there were other reasons for this. There must have been something about the person that made him or her unsuitable for more responsibility." They have no incentive to dig deeper, which is why most boards fail to defend Black professionals. The same people Blacks work with, work under, and must seek out for arbitration, mediation, and intervention are willfully blind to the problem. Black professionals are surrounded by parties not in their favor. While African Americans may have their own support networks through churches, mosques, fraternal orders, sororities, social and interest groups, and professional members groups and means of assistance, they still enter the ring alone when they are at work. The heavyweights in the C-suite treat them as featherweights to keep them in secondary or token positions, and they block their punches with silence and dismissal.

American commerce is rooted in slavery and the subservience of African Americans to Caucasians, so it is no surprise that African Americans who fight for the same prizes as whites are seen as troublemakers. Blacks who are complacent may receive token rewards, but those who push for full equality experience resistance and are often forced out of companies they significantly improved.

Often denial of executive promotions are not actual C-suite level executive or Board members' direct effrontery against Black professionals. Many times, it is the malice of the gatekeepers, who act more like overseers than mentors or supervisors to Black employees. The gatekeepers are the middle management or transition executives that work in educating and training as well as mentoring professionals in order to groom and prepare them for C-suite level positions. The gatekeepers often deem Black professionals unworthy versus the largely white candidates they favor for C-suite leadership. Black professionals continue to conform in an effort to fit the mold, but they are always outsiders. No matter how much positive change they lead or how consistently they rise within the company, they will still be denied access to the top floors of the organization.

By being demographically inconvenient to the organizational culture, Black professionals find themselves left out of conversations and initiatives that would speed their growth and better prepare them as candidates for higher positions. Companies must make a concerted effort to train and mentor Black professionals in the same ways they do for white candidates, or they will continue to work twice as hard while still being unprepared to compete with White candidates.

Corporate mentorship can provide exposure and a level of familiarity with upper management that instills comfort and confidence in African American employees. However, if a Blacks are not introduced to mentors or presented as potential leaders, they will continue to feel foreign and external and shrink from sharing perspectives that would benefit the company as a whole. The sooner Black professionals are provided exposure in a company, the better. When a firm is looking at candidates for C-suite positions, all Black candidates must be afforded access to all members of the deciding committee to assist in establishing rapport and familiarity.

Unfortunately, corporate culture still allows Blacks to be lumped into stereotypical categories that are based on caricatures rooted in slavery and economic abuse. When African Americans apply for a competitive position, all evidence of their merit, certification, awards, experiences, developments, publications, and studies is overlooked by senior white executives who feel more comfortable around white candidates who speak their language. The simple act of working while Black is threatening to the corporate elite, and African Americans continue to be perceived as invaders. The irony that repeats itself is that if not for African Americans, we would never have had an American economy that leads the world commercially and macroeconomically. The same people who were forced to build this great nation with whips across their backs and guns to their heads are treated as if their blood, sweat, and tears were somehow less of a contribution than that of those who held the whip.

Black executives must pretend not to see racial discrimination in key decisions, campaigns, investments, or programs established by white executive leaders that may be averse to African Americans and other communities of color. The scenario is no different when it comes to gender. When women enter a traditionally male-dominated executive administration or management team, they too are expected to act like men. However, white women are often allowed to hire other white women because they are seen as less of a threat to the status quo. This same threat-measurement is why there has been a trend to hire or place more Black women in positions of power than Black men. Black women are less of a perceived threat to the white patriarchy than Black men.

A leading concern that remains strong among many white executives is the fear that Black leadership will threaten the gains of whites. To date, there is no evidence of the disenfranchisement of white male stakeholders as a group within any firm or corporation. There has never been a hostile takeover by an Asian front, Latino rise in power, Native American gain, or Black shift in power. What has taken place is a shift in power that has generated opportunity by establishing and maintaining rights people have to access opportunity and excel in American society without facing illegal, immoral, or unfair challenges—considered traditional in many white hierarchal circles.

Black executives are made to feel uncomfortable in addressing things from a Black perspective or any perspective that embraces African American interests. It is evident that racism in corporate America, specifically in regard to C-suite executive positions, is not solely a social or political issue but a psychological issue of power and fear for many whites. They fear losing to an opponent that they have systematically weakened, because it would prove that they were not the heavyweights after all.

To move corporations past these archaic notions and unfounded fears, leaders need to stop repeating the cycle of racial abuse and transparently address any and all economic and cultural disconnects with their customers by employing a more diverse group to head their organizations. Meanwhile, white men who set aside opportunities for those who look and act like them must be taken down. To combat such agendas, Black professionals need to establish their value as assets to companies and draft their own social contracts that are non-negotiable and which directly equate to capital gain, organizational influence, promotions, and power.

This brings us back to the boxing ring, where the only way for the underdog to triumph is to use his opponent's strengths against him or her. Conformity to the rigged rules of the fight will not accomplish this. For decades, Black executives who try mightily to conform to white social norms have shown to be rewarded with nothing more than confusion, insults, and psychological. Using the strength of white-powered corporations to "re-right" the rules means allowing them to fail *because* of their myopic, homogenous viewpoints. Innovative companies will see the long-term benefit of diversity for communicating with and appealing to their customer bases. Those companies are the future, and Black executives will naturally gravitate towards them, bringing their talents and insights with them. Old-guard corporations that continue to operate like they are overseeing Black sharecroppers will quickly lose ground in this new economic reality.

In 1986, John deButts, former CEO of AT&T, once said, "Business needs Black executives with the courage and insight to help us understand issues involving equal opportunity. They must tell us what we need to know, not just what they think we want to hear" (Jones, 1986). Yet nearly 35 years later, nothing has changed to protect Black executives from the retaliation of white executives who make policy based on racial views or values. If Blacks are to win this fight, they must disempower their opponents by exposing their strengths as the weaknesses they are. White executives have tunnel vision that makes them comfortable in the corporate environment but foreign to their customers. Blacks can use this blind spot to their advantage, sweeping up disenfranchised consumers with every punch until they—the featherweights of the coporate —are the heavyweight champions of commerce.

WISDOM TO APPLY IN
THE CORPORATE RING:

• Training for this fight starts early on in most Black careers—sometimes even before a Black man or women is first hired. African Americans are turned away time and time again for having "Black sounding names," and they are intimidated in interviews by the white gaze.

• One of the most effective ways for Blacks to continue to punch above their weight class is to use their opponents' strengths against them. Whites by far have the greatest share of voice in American corporate leadership, so forcing them to voice their commitment—or lack of commitment—to diversity is a start.

• Many Black professionals are banding together with third-party allies to monitor which companies are hiring African Americans for advanced positions, specifically companies that claim they support Black promotion and progress.

• To enact real change, white corporate leaders must admit the problem is rooted in personal selections and skewed hiring practices. They must make a personal and professional investment in fostering diversity in order to see substantial growth. And they must stop requiring Black candidates to perform above their weight classes simply for a chance to compete.

• The more diverse American society becomes, the more companies that incorporate diversity into their business models will thrive. Recently, Proctor & Gamble (P&G) Chief Brand Officer, Mark Pritchard, stated that there is a need for the creative supply chain (i.e. brands, agencies, and production crews) to reflect the spectrum of target markets, specifically people of color, and he announced P&Gs commitment to multicultural representation

BOXING STRATEGY

FIGHT LIKE A WINNER

Don't waste time thinking about your mistakes and failures, and don't ever accept money to let someone else fight your battles. Championship boxers never quit and never accept defeat, and you shouldn't either.

ROUND 6

Step-Aside
MONEY

IN boxing, sometimes fighters are paid NOT to fight so that another boxer—usually a title holder—can avoid the embarrassment of being defeated and continue to dominate lesser opponents to maintain the façade of being a champion. Once this step-aside money is paid, and the better fighter foregoes a title-taking showdown in exchange for cash, the champion is free to pile on mediocre, paperweight fighters who have no real fighting ability or credibility. The titled fighter knows he can easily defeat weaker opponents with a few routine combinations, put on a good show for spectators and the media, then sit back and collect prize money. Therefore, paying a contender to walk away from the fight is a good investment. Though this seems like a simple business transaction, at its core, it is a gilded cage for a so-called champion who is afraid to give a worthy oponent a shot at taking his or her title. Meanwhile, the boxer who took the step-aside money has sold his shot at the title.

Eddie Hearn, head of Matchroom Boxing, once said, "If you believe in yourself, and you back yourself, you should never step aside. If you take step aside money, you're showing terrific weakness because you're giving someone an opportunity to take what you should feel is yours without you getting an opportunity to win it back."

In corporate America, step-aside money is paid for similar reasons. White executives and C-suite leaders are like paperweight champs who fear being knocked out by talented, hard-working, and established Black executives. To avoid the embarrassment of having to go toe-to-toe with a Black person, they will instead attempt to pay them—whether through hollow promises, offers to lead committees, or actual dollars—not to fight for inclusion in C-suite leadership. White leadership demands absolute loyalty and non-disclosure from Black executives who take step-aside money, which in essence, means they've stripped the Black executive of any chance to reach his or her potential and ensured that the executive will not complain or renege on the deal in the future.

White executives will pay step-aside money to protect their own positions and interests, but they also do it out of fear. They fear that Blacks will infiltrate their tight-knit, predominantly white-led, eventually flipping the leadership from predominantly white to non-white. They imagine how much harder they would have to legitimately win against driven, talented Blacks for administrative, financial, and operational C-Suite positions. Such positions are predominantly filled by whites because Blacks are routinely prevented from moving into them by intimidation and other tricks used to undermine and hamper Black advancement. But sabotaging Black executives takes much longer and is much riskier than simply incentivizing promising executives to step aside.

Black executives who accept step-aside money or rewards may do it consciously or unconsciously, but they eventually realize they have sabotaged their careers. It's purely a self-destructive act, and many think that by taking the "payment," or rather the "offer" they can't refuse, they will be rewarded for their loyalty, but the transaction is designed to benefit whites. A Black executive may take the bribe and be satisfied for a time, but when he or she realizes how limiting the agreement was, they become apathetic and eventually quit or are terminated. Black executives who take a payoff may change their minds about such agreements and demand more—more money, more power, and more influence, but because they have already been well-paid, they are easy to keep quiet and under control. Plenty of Black executives take a deal with the devil yet continue to throw don't-hit-me punches in an attempt to reassert their power. White leaders can perceive this as a breach of contract and respond with more aggressive tactics to regain control.

Black executives who continue to rock the boat after accepting step-aside money are often transferred to other departments or offered hefty severance packages so that white leaders can save face, save time, and save money, while ridding the corporation of a perceived threat to the status quo.

Before Black executives consider taking corporate bribes, they must realize they are taking a loss at the top. They are paid to fall. The fact they are paid at all means they had power. The original bribers are afraid of the Black executive as a contender, and they fear that they will lose their own power in a fair fight. When Black executives take payments that are significantly less valuable than what could be obtained through pain, patience, and perseverance, they often experience burnout, depression, and doubt as they look back over the smoldering ashes of a once red-hot career.

Rather than steppig aside and allowing white leaders to continue their domination in the corporate leadership ring, Black executives should train harder for the fights white leaders seek to avoid. When Blacks stop taking worthless bribes to avoid conflict, white leaders will stop offering them. They will know that their efforts to keep Blacks down will be apparent to their peers, the firm's stakeholders, the media, and even the U.S. Securities and Exchange Commission (SEC), which protects whistleblowers from ethical, commercial, technological, health-based, or sociopolitical violations under the Sarbanes-Oxley Act. These violations include efforts to undermine and negate the progression of Black leadership within a given organization.

When white leaders realize that a fair fight is inevitable and that a Black executive cannot be bought, their next move will be to pit the Black executive against "contenders" of other races to prove their commitment to diversity. Neither fighter will win in this scenario, but they will be redirected from the larger fight against white domination. It's as if white leaders are ancient Scythian kings announcing the Battle of the Minorities to begin in mortal combat! They use such tactics to distract from the fact that business as usual relies on the exclusion non-white perspectives.

Ultimately, it is corporate America that suffers when white leaders, in all of their mediocrity, hold Black executives at bay with step-aside money. When talented Blacks are robbed of their chance at a title or a seat at the table, corporations lose out on their perspectives, insights, and the raw determination to win.

Despite the fact that suppressing talent results in a loss to the corporation, white leaders continue to offer empty tokens and bribes because it works. Ever since white plantation owners learned to reward Black overseers for keeping common slaves in line, they have used loyalty and limited power as a weapon. Blacks sought the favor of white slave owners for survival and a modicum of comfort, but they really only gained a false sense of security. Black overseers paid for this feeling of security with continued subjugation and the knowledge that they betrayed their own. Some 157 years later, it's no longer a matter of life or death, but the result is the same. Black executives are paid to keep other minorities in line while gaining little ground in the fight for their own advancement.

Unfortunately, white leaders in corporate America have remained passive about creating real opportunities for Black men and women to take the helm, because it is easier to bait them with small rewards that incentivize them to help subjugate others.

Such tactics are deeply ingrained in American culture. No other race of people has been so freely exploited for the benefit of corporate elites. Yet, recent political shifts and calls for equality from the streets to the C-suites, are encouraging Black executives to own their worth and look at a bribes or step-aside money for what they are but turning down the step-aside bribes is easier said than done for those who feel they have no other options. Who wants to do daily battle against being ousted, unsupported, and completely out-maneuvered? There is little logic applied when generation after generation of Black professionals have been led to believe that by submitting to white culture, they will receive benefits that out-weigh the loss of self-respect and authentic Blackness. They may even believe that they are achieving against the odds.

Few Black icons have made it through the gauntlet of racial subjugation to gain control and power. In such cases, it is advantageous for racists to place such Black members in positions of power so they can still be overseen by whites so they can appear progressive without losing their position of dominance. How many Black executives who make it to the top still made deals that prevented them from fully taking the helm?

Black executives with any degree of power must stop taking step-aside money so that the next generation need not step down but can step up and ultimately force white corporate America to step off. We cannot allow white executives to buy and sell the hopes and dreams of Black executives or to shelve them like an item on layaway any longer. Rather, Blacks must understand their value as a bridge between the corporation and its customers, a large percentage of which are non-whites.

When Black business owners collaborate with white-led corporations, it is imperative that they seek agreements that are equally beneficial for all parties involved, however, there is a history of giving more than they get, which derails negotiations. White leaders want to use Black business owners for their access to resources, labor, and ideas, but they are not willing to provide adequate compensation. Instead, they act as if the Black professional should be grateful for their patronage and content with being included, even when it represents a loss.

The NFL is a prime example. While the institution continues to uphold racism in its practices, it needs Black talent to compete, so it creates token positions for Black executives to appear as a diverse organization. Unfortunately, those positions are few and far between. In 2020, there were only three Black head coaches and two Black general managers on the NFL's 32 teams even though 70% of the players are Black.

Thanks to a renewed interest in Black representation, the NFL administration has begun to press team owners to show more diversity in their front offices, though, there has been little change. NFL administrators and owners continue to hire white players as head coaches, regardless of their ability to lead, and it shows (Armour, 2021).

The NFL continues to hire white leaders with half as much experience, heart, and foresight as senior Black coaches with more experience in winning. Currently, there are fourteen openings for head coaches and general managers in the NFL, but the only man of color chosen to date is a Brown man, a Muslim man, named Robert Saleh chosen to be head coach of the New York Jets. white men still make up over 66% of the coaching staffs of NFL teams (Armour, 2021).

The underrepresentation is as insulting as it is mind-numbing. Nevertheless, white men who wish to dispel the idea that the NFL is racist, will point to the 2021 hiring of general managers Terry Fontenot of the Atlanta Falcons, Brad Holmes of the Detroit Lions, and Martin Mayhew of the Washington Football Team. They don't want to admit that the number of Black professionals can be counted on one hand and white general managers continue to be the majority, and they should not be the ones to decide if there is enough color in NFL.

There are many characters who appear to play both sides of the underrepresentation conflict in the NFL regarding general manager and head coach positions. Such characters are neither for nor against greater representation of color in higher level administrative or executive positions. For instance, Jeffrey Lurie, the owner of the Philadelphia Eagles, originally spearheaded efforts for greater diversification in the NFL through the league's Workplace Diversity Committee (WDC). Yet that effort did not help the very people it was intended to, making it moot. The Eagles haven't had a general manager or head coach of color for over 20 years. Ironic, indeed (Armour, 2021).

The NFL pulled a typical white executive move and hired Nick Sirianni, rather than Black coach Eric Bieniemy, as the offensive coordinator for the Indianapolis Colts. Though talented, Sirianni does not have the experience of transitioning good players into great champions. It is Bieniemy who has been recognized as the Master Yoda to Patrick Mahomes' Luke Skywalker, regarding Mahomes' development under Bieniemy's tutelage for three years as the offensive coordinator for the Kansas City Chiefs (Armour, 2021).

NFL administrators and owners deflect criticism by claiming that Blacks are a mismatch for certain teams, and they are simply selecting the right man for the job. But what defines the right man? Last time most people checked, winning games, having the respect of players and coaches throughout the league, and being an overall great person were the only true qualities that make a strong head coach. Nevertheless, Sirianni and so many like him, step to the front of the line, creating impediments for the advancement of Black and Brown men. From sports leagues to major media networks, the "bs"—biased situations—continue.

In 2018, CBS investigated their very own Leslie Moonves, a leading media executive, who resigned over his involvement in sexual harassment and racist activities that led to a non-conducive, hostile work environment (James, 2021). Further investigation led to similar discoveries about Peter Dunn, the president of CBS, and senior-level lieutenant, David Friend. These men consciously and viciously harassed and bullied women of all colors while specifically stopping Black journalists from ascending through the ranks or forcing them to resign. Moreover, Dunn and other senior-level executives within CBS led the $55-million purchase of a station in Long Island, New York so they could escape to a highly exclusive golf club located in the Hamptons. The deal even afforded one executive a $1-million golf membership. The money Dunn and his cronies used to reward themselves for a job poorly done, could have been invested in the hiring of qualified Black men and women and others of color. Fifty-six million dollars could have been invested in the station itself by improving staff, purchasing new technology, and ensuring a higher quality of news and entertainment to the masses, but no. White executives prove themselves willing to undermine the very nature and purpose of their own broadcasting companies for personal profit (James, 2021). Yet, they are still seen as preferable to Blacks who would work tirelessly to make money for the network rather than for themselves. How many qualified Black leaders were paid step-aside money so that these morally deficient white men could rob the corporation with virtual impunity? What is the point of such investigations when people like Peter Dunn continue in their positions, unfazed, feeling no remorse or embarrassment—and receiving no reprimand? (James, 2021).

Black executives must be mindful not to allow our message, our fight, to become defined by the misdeeds of white men. However, corporations must understand what they lose when they overlook Black professionals who are committed to driving a solid, strong, and stable organization.

Dunn's behavior was not a mistake or accident–it was entitlement. White men like him play these games knowing they are safe from reprimand solely because they are white. When CBS refused to make a bigger issue out of the scandal, they broke the solidarity they claim to have with the Black community, other communities of color, and white women.

CBS is no different than the thousands of companies who only focus on race and gender when they are called out on it. For instance, CBS decided to air the new drama, *The Equalizer*, starring Queen Latifah in 2021 as if to say, "See, diversity and inclusion. Now stop complaining." The message is that token gestures are enough, however, numbers are everything in business, and the fact is there are still only three Black professionals in highly visible positions at CBS.

It has been estimated that CBS has generated annual revenues in excess of $1.6 billion despite allegations of racism and sexism within the company. The behavior continues because greedy people simply look the other way and lie to themselves about what is ethical, professional behavior. CBS has a history of failed reforms that led to boycotts such as Reverend Jesse Jackson's boycott in 1986 over a Black journalist who was mistreated and demoted. In 2000, the U.S. Equal Employment Opportunity Commission (EEOC) received $8 million from CBS based on consistent reports of mistreatment of non-white employees and women of all colors (James, 2021). Moreover, it would be two years before legislation would protect whistleblowers from retaliation and further harassment for filing complaints against employers such as CBS—the Sarbanes-Oxley Act of 2002.

In 2015, Dunn sent veteran general manager, Brien Kennedy to manage various local CBS stations. Kennedy, unlike Dunn, but similar to Bob Bakish, sought to overhaul as many local CBS stations across the country as he could. Kennedy fired a number of mediocre white executives because he wanted to hire individuals that reflected the spectrum of demographics within the viewership. Afterall, viewership is what advertisers pay for. News networks by themselves create nothing. They do not even create the news they report. However, they provide a platform for advertisers that allows corporate America to sell everything from the latest video game console to nasal inhalant. Kennedy stressed that CBS couldn't compete with other networks if it didn't meet certain representation requirements to increase the viewership of news, shows, and events (James, 2021).

In late 2015, Kennedy and lead news director, Margaret Cronan, decided to hire Brooke Thomas as the lead news anchor for CBS Philadelphia. Neither Dunn nor his lieutenant, David Friend liked Thomas but still gave Kennedy and Cronan confirmation to hire her. Friend later turned on Cronan and Kennedy stating he despised Thomas professionally and personally. Friend demanded Thomas be fired. Both Kennedy and Cronan noted how Cronan suffered sexist abuse and was attacked for her support to hire more leading Black personalities in front and behind the camera. The idiocy of racism and sexism stood in the way of actual viewership for CBS Philadelphia. In 2016, Thomas' performance as a lead anchor led to higher viewership ratings at an increase of 20%. Nevertheless, Thomas was later terminated by Kennedy himself at the command of Friend and Dunn. Later, when contacted by the *Los Angeles Times*, Thomas declined to respond to the incident (James, 2021).

Friend attempted to somehow smooth over the outrage by stating that 45% of the on-air news staff at CBS Philadelphia were people of color. However, the nature and reason for Friend's response at the time was obviously hollow and rooted in attempting to placate the backlash against him and CBS overall. Cronan left CBS in 2017. She just couldn't take any more of the drama, lies, and manipulation that Dunn and Friend continued to commit. Yet, Kennedy remained, and he understood that representation led to greater revenues (James, 2021).

Increased inclusion equals increased income. Therefore, Kennedy decided to take Ukee Washington, news anchor of CBS Philadelphia, and place him as the lead evening anchor. However, was a CBS veteran of 30 years, so in the end, it wasn't terribly heroic on Kennedy's part, but it was the right thing to do. Nevertheless, the story of Washington ties directly into reasons why white traditionalists like Dunn need to be removed from such high-paying, powerful positions. It is not known, but it can be presumed, that Washington did his fair share of making silent agreements and even settling for step-aside money when guys like Dunn had the audacity to refer to him as a "jive guy always dancing." What kind of corny blaxploitation reference was Dunn repeatedly making toward Washington? Anyone with a sense of American culture can't explain away the fact that racists and misogynists smile in the face of their victims and still make money off of them. Yet, this is based on a system (James, 2021).

Alone, the Dunns of the world are like the Trumps of the world—nothing without a system of skewed checks and balances that favor disenfranchisement and marginalization of non-white and non-male people. Nevertheless, Washington was proactive and generated projects such as the entertaining and touching on-air production *Brotherly Love*, a series of heartfelt narratives from Philadelphia residents. Between Dunn and his flunkies, racial insults bounced around board room meetings and emails, yet Washington prevailed at least for himself. Unfortunately, despite the attacks, Washington refused to respond to the *Los Angeles Times* when they conducted an interview of key CBS personnel involved in whistleblowing on bigots such as Dunn (James, 2021).

Currently, only two people of color—men of color—are general managers out of the 17 major market local CBS stations. These men are Tom Canedo of the Atlanta CW station and Brandin Stewart of CBS Philadelphia. Canedo is Latino; Stewart is Black. CBS was retaliation, little to nothing happened (James, 2021).

The entire CBS Philadelphia ordeal is a clear example of white male traditionalism that perverts and poisons the very presentation of so-called facts in news. How can people of any demographic receive objective news coverage when it is clearly slanted by white males solely as the source of power, privilege, and, in this case, information? They can't. Considering the efforts of Cronan and Kennedy to battle Dunn and Friend, it is evident that there is an internal war that continues between white progressives, liberals and white traditionalist conservatives, beyond the floors of Congress, the Oval Office, or the U.S. Supreme Court.

Most of the Black anchors and other essential staff simply

would not respond or comment to the *Los Angeles Times* regarding the racism and racialized sexism they suffered while working with CBS, and in particular with CBS Philadelphia under Dunn and Friend. This is a powerful example of the step-aside mentality Dunn and others like him anticipate. Is it out of fear or self-preservation—or is it just a matter of stepping aside and going along with the "bs"--business as usual because it is easier to do than fighting? Whatever drives Blacks to step-aside rather than rise up and fight, their silence represents wasted opportunities. Even if more Black men and women are hired to leadership positions in media, business, or politics, it means nothing if they won't directly confront racism and racialized sexism within the corporation.

It's time that Black executives and others in influential positions take a stand as top-ranking contenders against the paperweight champions and stop taking bribes or agreeing to look the other way. If they don't, then the progression of Black people, as a whole, will continue to be compromised.

"

*Black executives
must be mindful
not to allow our
message, our fight,
to become defined
by the misdeeds
of white men.*

"

WISDOM TO APPLY IN
THE CORPORATE RING:

• Eddie Hearn, head of Matchroom Boxing, once said, "If you believe in yourself, and you back yourself, you should never step aside. If you take step aside money, you're showing terrific weakness because you're giving someone an opportunity to take what you should feel is yours without you getting an opportunity to win it back."

• White executives will pay step-aside money to protect their own positions and interests, but they also do it out of fear. They fear that Blacks will infiltrate their tight-knit, predominantly white-led corporation, eventually flipping the leadership from predominantly white to non-white.

• Ultimately, it is corporate America that suffers when white leaders, in all of their mediocrity, hold Black executives at bay with step-aside money. When talented Blacks are robbed of their chance at a title or a seat at the table, corporations lose out on their perspectives, insights, and the raw determination to win.

• Black executives with any degree of power must stop taking step-aside money so that the next generation need not step down but can step up and ultimately force white corporate America to step off. We cannot allow white executives to buy and sell the hopes and dreams of Black executives or to shelve them like an item on layaway any longer. Rather, Blacks must understand their value as a bridge between the corporation and its customers, a large percentage of which are non-whites.

• Whatever drives Blacks to step-aside rather than rise up and fight, their silence represents wasted opportunities. Even if more Black men and women are hired to leadership positions in media, business, or politics, it means nothing if they won't directly confront racism and racialized sexism within the corporation.

BOXING STRATEGY

PLAY MIND GAMES

Bobbing and weaving is all about catching your opponent off guard. Playing mind games can have the same effect. Smile at your opponent, hold one hand behind your back or do pushups between rounds like Bernard Hopkins II in his fight against Jean Pascal. Mental games make your opponent look foolish, and they can break them down without landing a punch.

Bobbing and
WEAVING

Bobbing and weaving are defensive maneuvers used in boxing to avoid punches while moving closer in on the opponent. If an opponent throws a left hook, a fighter will drop down and move his or her head to the right to prevent the hit from landing. Boxers like Mike Tyson use bobbing and weaving to remove their opponent's immediate target while positioning themselves for a better opportunity to counterpunch. This technique is only effective when the fighter keeps his or her weight centered and grounded to avoid going off balance and becoming an easier target.

In corporate America, Black executives turn to bobbing and weaving to escape the non-stop blows coming their way. They, too, must maintain balance and uphold their original stance to keep from being thrown off balance and making themselves an even bigger target. Whether in boxing or in corporate America, how a person executes bobbing and weaving tactics often has to do with whether he or she is fighting out of fear or fighting to win.

Black executives who want to win must understand the need to adhere to their decisions and maintain their stances no matter what. It is the fear of making mistakes, fear of the potential reprimand, and fear of what white leaders might do, that shakes Black executives to the core and causes them to lose their balance. When a boxer walks into the ring fearful of losing (and at times even looking too lose), he or she is fighting out of fear. A champion stays laser-focused on the goal of winning despite knowing there's a good chance of a knockout. This is an act of sheer bravery—a life skill learned more often in the streets than in the Ivy League.

Facing an opponent while remaining firmly grounded, requires fighters to react fluently, alternating between strategic offense and defense. Strategic, because offensively throwing long, wild jabs and hooks leaves a boxer open to a counterpunch that could come as a body shot. In such a position, retreating only places the boxer in a confined position, losing the mobility to face the attack. A strong boxer must understand how to anticipate what an opponent will do based his or her size, speed, agility, precision, endurance, and location in the ring. Distance can be used defensively, but also—forcing the opponent to walk into a wall of head-knocking blows.

Boxers and Black executives—can't punch all the time. The human body can only exert so much force and motion at one time unless the motion is repetitious and, even then, there is a point where they hit a plateau. Likewise, simply taking punches increases the potential for a fatal punch to land. Staying in motion while also maintaining a strong stance is difficult, but it is an absolute necessity for those hoping to win a title fight. Techniques like the rope-a-dope in which a fighter covers up and leans back against the ropes, allowing the opponent to exhaust him or herself by throwing punches, can only be executed well if a fighter knows how to bob and weave while staying centered.

The 1974 Rumble in the Jungle boxing event between Muhammad Ali and George Foreman is infamous for how Ali purposely backed himself up against the ropes and withstood a hail of blows before delivering a fight-winning knockout in the eighth round. Ali used this move, aptly named the rope-a-dope, against Foreman because he had no choice. He was too old to spend eight rounds bobbing and weaving to avoid being knocked out by an undefeated world heavyweight champion, and the event was held in Kinshasa, Zaire, where the heat and humidity were overwhelming. Because he could not sustain the continuous movement needed to counter his hard-punching opponent, Ali introduced the rope-a-dope. But for that strategy to work, he had to commit to taking punches, and he had to rely on his own ability to stay centered and find his opening. Ali was a 4-1 underdog when he went into the ring that night, and yet he regained his title in front of 60,000 people and invented a new boxing tactic along the way.

What this story tells us is that when you are an underdog in a fight, staying centered, prepared, and having a few tricks up your sleeve can be the difference between certain defeat or career-changing victory. Ali was not afraid to lose this fight. Even as the older underdog, he entered the ring ready to win. This fight was a prime example of how an outmatched fighter can use defensive tactics offensively to confuse and overwhelm an opponent.

Footwork is key to the success of such tactics. By keeping an opponent on his or her toes and wary of what combination will be thrown next, a strategic boxer can quickly turn the tables and leave everyone—including his or her opponent—wondering what just happened. Bobbing and weaving is a dance of sorts, and the fighter must know how to coordinate the upper torso with the movement of his or her feet. While the technique is considered defensive, it is used to expose the opponent's weakness, providing the opportunity for a body shot or head shot. It is also a means to get as close as possible to the opponent and undo his or her skill. In this position, the opponent loses the ability to properly land punches and exposes him or herself to the boxer's impending counterattack. The trick is never to stop outmaneuvering the opponent, because bobbing and weaving can quickly be stopped with a stiff jab, an overhand right or left cross, or the unseen-until-it's-too-late uppercut. A boxer who bobs and weaves must keep his or her focus on the opponent, moving closer and closer, while avoiding being hit or, at times, brushing the brunt of a fist aside. Then when the boxer finds opportunity... Boom! The boxer attacks, landing the winning punch. With such force, focus, and freedom, the boxer cuts through the opponent's offense and sends the opponent into defensive mode. Once the opponent yields either space or time, the boxer can take the upper hand and move in for the win.

When bobbing and weaving in the corporate environment,

Black executives should adhere to the same principles. Quick thinking is more useful than deep thinking. Simply having one's feet planted but not reinforcing the stance, leaves one vulnerable to being knocked down or simply tripping and falling. Black executives must be flexible, adaptable, and learn to build their own networks outside of their company walls to gain the support they need to withstand punches.

White executives often attempt to disenfranchise and silence Black executives by questioning the validity of their ideas, strategies, campaigns, years of experience, areas of expertise, and even the very universities where they received their degrees. When those areas are exhausted, then it becomes a matter of making the Black executive look like a clueless or selfish upstart or tenured executive set on leading the company down a path of loss in the short term or long term. The fear that somehow a Black executive's ideas will lead to loss for white executives, raises alarms when there is nothing to fear. White executives will exhaust themselves trying to disqualify Black ideas from consideration, sending the clear message to Black executives that they lost the minute they stepped into the ring, and no amount of bobbing and weaving will help. Here is where the Black executive must consider flexibility and adaptability—how to bob and weave around a fallacious argument posed by an opponent bent on undermining the Black executive's support and strategy.

Black executives can turn the tables on white leaders by focusing on why the onslaught is taking place and not on how best to defend one's ideas, concepts, or campaigns. By doing this, Black executives highlight the vehemence behind white leaders' attempts at dismantling Black credibility. It is not that white executives never attack each other's ideas, but they rarely attack the character or integrity of an opposing executive directly. However, when Black and white executives clash, white opposition seems to focus on the executive's Blackness itself, making it suspect, rather than accepting opposing viewpoints.

Thanks to Black Lives Matter and other unapologetic movements aimed at gaining Black equality, corporate America is at a turning point. Firms are now attempting to put distance between their racist past and the current wave of public intolerance for racism and sexism in the workplace. Today, white traditionalists are relics of a bygone era in which it is acceptable to devalue and deny rights to men and women simply because of the color of their skin. Removing those dinosaurs is far more difficult when they remain at the helm of the corporate ship and can easily distract from their own dark-handed tactics.

Therefore, before considering retaliation, legal action, or protests, Black executives must know, and know how, to illuminate the underhanded tactics whites use to maintain the upper hand. Bobbing and weaving—or slipping out from behind a punch before it lands—underscores the attempted punch itself. Why was it thrown? How hard was it thrown? And how much company time and resources are being wasted on trying to defeat someone who is supposed to be on your team just because he or she is Black?

Cheryl Grace is not a boxer, but she has fought like a champion during her time as a Black executive in corporate America. She literally fought her way to the top by gracefully bobbing and weaving against racist, sexist opponents. Her career became national news when she was pitted against David Kenney, CEO and Chief Diversity Officer at Nielsen Global Media, a company that measures audience engagement through ratings metrics used across all channels and platforms from podcasts to streaming TV to social media.

Grace was well-received at Nielsen, and she rose through the ranks by leaps and bounds. Even though she experienced instances of racialized sexism, the clashes were minor compared to her clash with David Kennedy (Hartman, 2021). Grace was known for being a stellar employee and a progressive when it came to researching underrepresented populations of color, specifically African Americans. Grace organized a transfixing body of market research regarding Black consumer trends. The research established that African Americans generate $1.5 trillion per year (Hartman, 2021; Statista, 2021; Tucker, 2017)—dollars that make them a valuable consumer demographic. Grace convinced the predominantly white male executive team to recognize opportunities advertisers were missing by not marketing directly to African Americans. Through Grace's leadership, the executives incorporated her ideas and began communicating the need for growth in this area.

There's nothing revolutionary about the idea that marketing to African American consumers leads to more opportunities, greater profits, and increased brand loyalty. In fact, it's just logical. But for the white leaders at Nielsen who had not transitioned out of the "white is right" mentality, it was downright radical thinking. The only way Grace could make her ideas palatable was to appeal to their greed. As they say, money moves morals. Companies like Nielsen may claim they proactively promote inclusive workplace environments, yet they cling to remnants of slavery. Today, the form of enslavement is no longer involuntary labor, it is voluntary consumerism. These corporations want Black money, but they resist the idea of giving Blacks too much power, especially within their own walls. Yet Grace used what power she had to advocate for positive representation for African American consumers by pushing Nielsen to support more programming produced by African Americans. This allowed Blacks to express their own unadulterated, "un-Eurocentrized" presentations of Black experiences in America. In this situation, Grace was not bobbing and weaving to avoid punches, she was offensively punching through barriers to elevate her vision and Black people like her.

At first, Grace was successful. For a time, Nielsen consented to focus on the need for broadcasters to specifically market to Black consumers on social media and other digital platforms.

Based on Grace's ideas, Nielsen provided broadcasting, advertising, and social media networks information highlighting the most profitable areas for reaching Black consumers. These areas included cosmetics, hair and beauty products, and women's stockings. In 2004, Grace was made the Vice President of Communications and Community and was then made Senior Vice President of U.S. Strategic Community Alliances and Consumer Engagement (Hartman, 2021). Cheryl Grace was an icon leading a progressive front from the top of Nielsen's power structure.

THEN DAVID KENNEY
became the CEO.

The very white-minded Kenney was assigned as Nielsen's Chief Diversity Officer. Unlike Grace, Kenney was not interested in improving Black representation in media, and he was fixated on spending no more than 10% of the budget to address diversity and inclusion issues. Diversity and inclusion is the top social justice issue for revolutionary development in American business, politics, and society overall. Nevertheless, it was evident Kenney didn't really care, and Nielsen's stock suffered by a decrease of 26% (Hartman, 2021). Kenney continued to meet Grace's punches with forceful, bigoted counterpunches, even though it resulted in decreased profits.

Grace persisted by bobbing and weaving in response to Kenney's attack, but he went on the offensive again after a meeting in which Grace spoke about her insights as a Black woman raised in Black communities. She stood behind her research, centered in racial disparities. Grace stated workers of color, and specifically Black employees, were worked like modern slaves with no road to promotion and no sense of real progression. In a letter, Grace proposed solutions to address the drop in the budget from $7.5 million to $117,000 in addition to the workforce reduction (Hartman, 2021).

Kenney obviously felt Grace had returned his counterpunch with a left-handed uppercut. The actions he took following that letter, showed that he saw Grace as a dangerous opponent. He soon pushed Grace against the ropes by patronizing her "big ideas" and asking her to meet with him privately to discuss the matters further. But that meeting never happened. Instead, Grace received disturbing calls from both the legal and human resources departments at Nielsen asking her if she was interested in a severance package. Grace was in shock and disbelief that Kenney fired her without any notice. (Hartman, 2021). Obviously, Grace was furious—Kenney had stunned her with a right hook that came out of nowhere. What was her quickest means to recover?

Grace filed a lawsuit in Federal Court on the grounds of racial discrimination, and though the case has not been adjudicated, the evidence remains in her favor. Again, Cheryl Grace is a clear example of the use of bobbing and weaving to tire out opponents so that she can counterpunch effectively. Kenney apparently was not expecting to face a public lawsuit. These are trying times for white racists who refuse to redeem themselves in America (Hartman, 2021).

In 2021, Cheryl Grace resigned from Nielsen.
She left to establish her executive coaching and consulting business, "I Am Cheryl Grace." Grace's business is under Grace's lifestyle brand Powerful Penny LLC.
Grace and Kenney exchanged formalities obviously regarding an undisclosed agreement.

Kenney addressed Grace's strength in promoting and improving awareness of systemic racism, racialized sexism, and the need for greater opportunity for professionals of color within Nielsen.

Chase used the opportunity to list her achievements while working at Nielsen and thanked the company for her senior leadership experience to better the company by focusing on communities of color and their influence (Grace, 2021).

African American women like Grace have learned to expertly execute bobbing and weaving tactics out of necessity. Black women have greater success than Black men securing positions with C-suites and in non-profits, but they often face fierce opponents once they get there. One of the best-known CEOs of a non-profit interest group is Jo Ann Jenkins of AARP. Since 2010, Jenkins has led that organization as an advocate for American senior citizens. As a Black woman, it is certain that Jo Ann Jenkins overcame the same opposition that so many other Black women face but just allowing her in the ring is considered a victory.

Sadly, only 13% of Black women with MBAs make it to the executive level versus 45% of their white counterparts with the same degree (McQueen, 2020). Statistics like this one have sparked debates about whether white women should be considered minorities. When a white woman is hired over a Black woman with similar or greater credentials, it's not hard to see that the white woman is benefitting from white privilege. She is favored as an executive because she is more likely to uphold the white patriarchy that is rooted in Southern slavery, New England elitism, and fantasies of Manifest Destiny throughout the West. White women have historically fed into it by accepting "second-in-command" positions as docile wives on plantations, plasticine First Ladies, and powerful but less-than positions within corporate America. White women thrive because they inadvertently uphold the power structure even as they benefit from it, and white men need them to create an illusion of inclusion.

It's hard to believe that white patriarchy still thrives in corporate America when white men make up just 35% of the American population. Their tyranny continues because of the role each player is willing to play. White women are told they are strong and progressive, but they are expected to settle for less in exchange for being allowed to participate. Too often, they agree to this role in exchange for a modicum of power. For Black executives, the bargain cuts deeper. Both Black men and women are made to feel indebted when they are hired or promoted. Every time the powers that be accept a Black idea, they praise the Black executive as if they are throwing a bone to a dog. They give talented Black executives scraps as if from the leftover holiday dinner, the plantation owner just devoured. They seem to say, "Enjoy it, because it is not likely to come around again soon." Being given scraps in exchange for money-making ideas looks something like this:

Even though, the upward mobility of Black women increased in the 1990s, surpassing that of Black men, they represent less than 1% of for-profit corporations, and in some reports less than 2% of non-profits. African American women account for just 7% of the leadership workforce in corporate America. Only Coca-Cola, Starbucks, and Walmart have significant levels of African American women in leading executive roles (McQueen, 2020, 4, 5, 8).

Against these odds, some Black women bob and weave by acting "whiter" or making strategic moves that are deemed Eurocentric. Subjugating themselves to white coercion in this way is, in boxing terms, losing their stance. Remember, the only rule in bobbing and weaving is that the fighter maintain his or her stance, preventing themselves from losing balance and becoming an easier target. There are people who would call whitewashing oneself selling out, but it is actually just a sign of poor form. The fighter has lost her stance because she is too focused on not losing. The underlying effort is not an act of disloyalty against her own race, but an inability to succeed any other way.

Another area that knocks Black women off balance is the expectation that they will submit to secondary or assistant positions, even when they have the talent and drive to do the bigger job themselves. Kamala Harris is a perfect example of this. She could not win the White House as a Black woman (that would have been a double revolution!), so she now plays second fiddle to a white executive as VOTUS, the Vice President of the United States. Many of us are proud to call her Madame Vice President as she serves the Nation, but even as the second most powerful leader in the world, Vice President Harris will have to do a lot more bobbing and weaving to make her real dreams come true.

Both Black men and women find themselves on the ropes when they ignore continuous and blatant acts of racism and racialized sexism in the workplace. Eventually, they either have to throw a punch or retire from the ring. Black executives employ several strategies to escape this dangerous position. One strategy is to overcompensate in areas they believe fit social norms. They do this to protect their personal narrative, highlight their skills, and steer clear of stereotypes such as being the angry Black woman or aggressive Black man. The problem with this strategy is that they are already on the ropes, so when they allow their opponent to tire themselves out, they are resigning themselves to the beating.

Another strategy Black men and women employ is staying calm when they are angry. Corporate leaders may read this stance as docile and subservient—or even slow—but the reality is Black people see humbling oneself in the face of aggression as a virtue. It is a tactic they have learned from hundreds of years of swallowing pride and biting their tongues to survive the evils of slavery and servitude. This stance does not serve them well in a corporate environment that values assertiveness and strength, but it would be equally problematic for them to be tagged as an angry Black person and quickly find themselves out of a job.

One way around this conundrum is to appeal to what matters to white executives more than maintaining white privilege. The answer, of course, is money. When Black executives show an impact on the bottom line or help improve the company's relationship with the public and primary target markets, they make themselves indispensable. Until they aren't.

When bad press and potential lawsuits arise because of the racist acts of whites like David Kenney, corporations run for cover. Often, they react with an image makeover and attempt to change in their stated policies to make it seem as if they are champions of diversity among stakeholders. By doing this, they can avoid addressing the acts of white executives directly and instead, paint the Black executive as emotionally sensitive, presumptuous, or a "reverse" racist. Even when Black executives seek the support of human resources, most investigations do not lead to direct retaliation against the Black executive, otherwise, there is a violation of the Sarbanes-Oxley Act of 2002, and the lawsuits can begin. For this reason, even when there is blatantly racist or racialized sexism at work, Black men and women often choose to bob and weave while remaining diplomatic versus combative. The only time direct response comes in the form of a counterattack is when they are out of options.

The final strategy Blacks use to stay in the ring is to avoid personal disclosures about their perspectives, experiences, and backgrounds. In this sense, Black men and women hide their own worldviews and create separate business personas. This can be perceived as a caricature of who they actually are, and it makes them suspect to white leaders. But Black executives are wary of having information they share used against them, and for good reason. Many Black executives feel they will be giving white executives ammunition against them when they disclose personal information, so they sit in silence as they endure "my Black friend" speeches from white colleagues. The "my Black friend" speech is when a culturally ignorant or racist white person selects a Black person as the archetype upon which all Black people are measured. This is a racial play that allows white people to own the narrative that rightly belongs to Black executives. The diversity among people of African descent is greater anthropologically than many European cultures. Yet, the assumption of many whites is that all Blacks are African Americans. When a Black executive attempts to explain the underlying diversity behind the term "Black," they are met with "my Black friend" stories.

When a Black executive accepts the whitewashed characterization of Blacks, he or she becomes a puppet of the system, a puppet of the executives that put the Black executive in power. By doing and saying nothing to enrage white colleagues, the Black executive maintains the very system of leadership that attempts to silence Black representation and leadership itself. The Black executive is thus made a token, an agent of subjugation and oppression versus incorporation and advancement (Yancy, 2016).

Some corporations have begun to recognize the need for Blacks to be allowed in the ring, even if the fight is still less than fair. JP Morgan Chase was steeped in white traditionalist leadership for decades until 2016 when the corporation founded its Advancing Black Leaders Strategy, which specifically created a pipeline to identify and recruit Black employees into higher level management and administrative positions. Though not terribly awe-inspiring, one innovation worthy of focus is that the strategy is separate from the company's diversity and inclusion department, and the Advancing Black Leaders Strategy is C-Suite supported. Another example of companies recognizing the value of Black leadership can be found in Germany's multinational SAP. SAP's Black Employee Network entered a partnership with Delaware State University. The partnership, Project Propel, assists in training students from historically Black colleges and universities (HBCUs) in the business (Roberts & Mayo, 2019). Initiatives like these are a step in the right direction, but they fail to address the bobbing and weaving Blacks must do to stay in the ring once they get there.

One way for Blacks to keep their stance solid in the ring is to obtain a mentor as soon as possible. At every level of development, mentors provide insight that can impact decisions when faced with adversity. Over time, mentors at companies help to navigate and circumvent certain obstacles or to pursue and attain certain —specifically when facing white opposition. The most effective mentors for Black executives are other Black leaders who have successfully battled white-is-right thinking. Through a strong network of Black mentors and mentees, an individual can extend his or her resources, strategies, and tools and stay in the ring longer. According to a study, Black Harvard MBAs who ascended to executive positions (13% women, 19% men) stated their success was due to a group of mentors (Roberts & Mayo, 2019).

Not only does Black leadership increase a company's profit margin, it expands the general target market based not only on Black executives but greater emphasis and investment in the Black community. In 2008, Senator and soon-to-be-President Barak Obama said, "Change will not come if we wait for some other person or if we wait for some other time. We are the ones we've been waiting for. We are the change that we seek" (Roberts & Mayo, 2019). Therefore, bobbing and weaving is a matter of maintaining the fight long enough for the next generation to learn, train, and bridge the gap even further. Nonetheless, the mentor is only as valuable if his or her actions help the mentee pursue and maintain an executive/senior executive (C-suite) position. Historically, Black access to such positions has been limited by so-called white allies who prefer to reserve such positions for those who look like them. Regardless of company policy, white executives will always find ways to uphold the same racist and sexist infrastructure in which Black women and men need to seek some form of white patronage to succeed. This must stop. Unfortunately, business is still about who you know versus what you know. Corporations that sincerely want diversity, need to add meat to the bones of their Diversity and Inclusion departments to help non-white employees fight in higher weight classes.

Diversity and Inclusion departments may be charged with balancing racial inequity and social injustice, but they do far too little for Black people. Instead, Diversity and Inclusion departments are used to address the issues of non-Black employees, leaving little time or energy for those they are supposed to serve.

Often corporations support hiring and training African Americans, but they are largely absent when it comes to training and mentoring Black professionals. The biggest area of support Black professionals need as they bob and weave through corporate America is on how to counterpunch their way out of middle management. Mentorship should not end until the Black professional is a senior executive, at which point, he or she should receive developmental support from his or her peers, internal or external to the company. This shift will ensure greater enrichment and emergence of Black leadership in corporate America.

One way to do this is to move away from focusing on racial-sensitivity courses, and instead, focus on greater incorporation of African Americans in all aspects of leadership within the organization. In addition, D&I departments should make it a mission to support significant interaction between Black executives and C-suite leadership. This can operationalize the corporate vision of greater solidarity with the Black community and increase the number of Black executives who feel valued by the company. D&I should also be focused on making inclusion authentic. The one-size-fits-all, colorblind approach championed in the 1970s and 1980s failed because it did not recognize the value of difference. Black executives who thought they were accepted into the C-suite ranks because of their unique perspectives quickly learned that the bobbing and weaving intensifies when white leaders challenge their own inauthentic, stereotypical models of good, Black employees. It is the authentic Black executive's job to expose this flawed view and stand as a correction to the error and irony that white executives continue to propagate about Black leadership (Sisco, 2020; Roberts & Mayo, 2019).

Black executives must avoid placating white notions that Black leaders are an extension of white leadership and are only there to provide support. Such arrangements are an affront to Black authenticity and integrity, and they prevent Black leadership from gaining a foothold. white executives have a tendency to treat Black executives like vassals who serve the king, they feel Blacks owe them for their executive positions. Owing means the Black executive must maintain the status quo agenda that was designed to uphold white male values, excluding other perspectives.

Black executives should never embrace the strategy of working with their heads down and not objecting to anything the general administration does. Black executives should not need to cater to white executives to get ahead. When Black executives take on a high-stakes assignment, they need the resources to recruit, organize, and lead a team of their own making rather than being expected to micromanage a group of disorganized employees who are ill-equipped to successfully meet the assigned goal. Black executives should never work alone unless the assignment demands it. They must insist that they have the resources to succeed. From that point, it's a matter of being a leader and drawing individuals together in a self-supportive, intricate team ready to perform collaboratively together (Sisco, 2020).

Black executives perfect the art of bobbing and weaving because they have a target on their backs that grows as they rise in power. They are constantly dodging the blows of cultural or racial stereotypes that many white executives accept as truth. Black professionals report that they are regularly interrogated by white executives who view African American employees as a faceless, nameless workforce. Bobbing and weaving may help Blacks stay in the ring for a time, but to combat stereotypes with authentic Black leadership, Black executives will eventually have to go toe-to-toe to get what they want. Corporations that want to see true diversity must accept that the fight can and will turn ugly. Robust D&I departments can help ensure that Black executives have someone in their corner when this happens.

WISDOM TO APPLY IN
THE CORPORATE RING:

- In corporate America, Black executives turn to bobbing and weaving to escape the non-stop blows coming their way. They, too, must maintain balance and uphold their original stance to keep from being thrown off balance and making themselves an even bigger target. Whether in boxing or in corporate America, how a person executes bobbing and weaving tactics often has to do with whether he or she is fighting not to lose or fighting to win.

- Quick thinking is more useful than deep thinking. Simply having one's feet planted but not reinforcing the stance, leaves one vulnerable to being knocked down or simply tripping and falling. Black executives must be flexible, adaptable, and learn to build their own networks outside of their company walls to gain the support they need to withstand punches.

- One way for Blacks to keep their stance solid in the ring is to obtain a mentor as soon as possible. At every level of development, mentors provide insight that can impact decisions when faced with adversity. Over time, mentors at companies help to navigate and circumvent certain obstacles or to pursue and attain certain opportunities—specifically when facing white opposition.

- Black executives must avoid placating white notions that Black leaders are an extension of white leadership and are only there to provide support. Such arrangements are an affront to Black authenticity and integrity, and they prevent Black leadership from gaining a foothold.

- Corporations that want to see true diversity must accept that the fight can and will turn ugly. Robust D&I departments can help ensure that Black executives have someone in their corner when this happens.

BOXING STRATEGY

TRAP THEM IN THE ROPES OR CORNER

When you're going toe-to-toe against a worthy opponent, controlling the ring is paramount. Pushing your opponent back onto the ropes or into a corner is one of the easiest ways to throw them off because most boxers are most comfortable in the center of the ring. When you take control, you rob your opponent of control, which is the first step toward victory.

ROUND 8

Going
TOE TO TOE

In the 1800s, boxing was a sport mainly reserved for the elite and gentlemen of means were the only ones who could afford formal boxing lessons. This is why boxing is often referred to as a gentleman's sport. Boxers remain upright throughout a bout, using only their fists as weapons, and the rules prohibit them from using elbows, head-butting their opponents, or relying on other low-blows. Boxers are not allowed to hit the nape, back of the head, or below the belt, and they must cease fighting when an opponent is on the ground. All of these rules make boxing appear to be a polite sport when compared with, say, American football or mixed martial arts. But this perception is far from the truth. Boxing can be brutal, and boxers must be aggressive, determined, and unforgiving to go toe-to-toe and win.

The strict rules of boxing do have one effect, boxers must control their emotions, or they could lose the fight on a technicality. To engage, survive, and win a toe-to-toe fight, a boxer must shed all bad habits that might be used to win on the street, but lead to certain defeat in the ring. Boxers simply can't win through sheer brutality or force alone. Defense is critical to their success. The smart boxer must maintain a solid defense while acting on offense, because once boxers stop thinking about protecting themselves, drop their gloves, fail to bob and weave, fail to recover, or stand winded and panting—POW! They may take a straight jab to the face followed by an uppercut that leaves the boxer in a cloud of uncertainty as the referee starts counting down.

When Black executives go toe-to-toe against the powers that be in corporate America, they would be smart to adopt this same approach. Unfortunately, many cling to strategies that do not work and lead to repeated failure. This lack of discipline often stems from fear. Some Black executives are so fearful of losing what little they've been given by white-led corporations, they pull punches, fail to cover themselves, or react in an unseemly manner out of weakness rather than strength. Such reactions give corporations control over the flow of the fight, and when it eventually wears down the boxer, leaders are free to change up their fighting style and go for the knockout.

Unfortunately, adhering to the rules is not always possible for Black executives, because the rules of engagement in corporate culture are different for different people, making fighting while Black a considerable disadvantage. Black executives may see white leaders hit below the belt and think it is fair game. They only find out they are wrong when they are reprimanded or dismissed. If, over time, they manage to decipher the unspoken rule that white is might and might is right, they may adopt a more defensive posture and avoid throwing punches to remain in the ring. Even if these fighters are disciplined enough to shed their bad habits, their opponents never will. This is why they must tap into the fighting spirit.

The fighting spirit demands that a boxer tighten up his or her skills. The same goes for Black executives who may be naturally assertive—an asset in corporate America—but are portrayed by the opposition as irrational, emotional, misinformed, or merely combative and contrary. Rather than falling for the bait, Black executives must exude determination and avoid being distracted by minor jabs meant to ridicule or belittle them. Black executives are held to a higher standard of conduct, so they must overcome corporate opponents through will and drive alone.

Black executives who want to prevail in this unfair fight, must realize the bout is do or die and learn to rely on their own drive. The drive to win against all odds is often fueled by intuition and experience. By the time Black executives finish the long climb to corporate leadership, they begin to move like heavyweight champions. They react to racist maneuvers quickly and without a second thought, acting from muscle memory and the intuitive ability to anticipate an attack. Over time, successful Black executives realize what works and what doesn't. Will an emotional approach be a strength or weakness? Is a more cerebral approach received with support or skepticism? How will the members of the administration respond in the short-term and long-term to how a Black executive responds to challenges and obstacles presented by white traditionalist opposition?

Some senior Black executives choose to throw away the

crutches for good and dive right into the fray. Like a prize-fighting boxer, the Black executive never thinks, "What if this safety net splits? What if my strategy proves to be unstable, and the foundation I stand on collapses?" He or she doesn't buy into the potential of a loss but fights to win. Senior Black executives gain this inner strength by understanding that they can win with what they have. It's the self-imposed hindrances and obstacles that lead most Black executives to succumb to a silent agreement. It is the fear of losing everything. Senior Black executives have realized that if they give their power away, they have nothing left to lose.

Black executives have unique talents and strengths that corporations need. That is why they were hired. They need to realize that they do not owe blind loyalty or a willingness to play second fiddle to whites in order to maintain the respect of their peers. Instead, they gain respect by not folding to the powers that be and not accepting veiled threats as inevitable job loss.

While some Black executives make silent agreements in exchange for promises that they believe will pay off over time, senior Black executives know that it's not worth the gamble. When a Black executive—or a boxer, for that matter—banks on the hope that an opponent will display some sort of sportsmanship, they've lost the game. In a fight, there is no room for true etiquette. No one ever hands a victory to his or her opponent out of kindness. Black executives hoping the opposition will more or less take it easy on them are asking for trouble. The opposition will not.

Black executives do not owe anyone for their accomplishments and must realize the opposition can't take anything away unless they allow it. The most common way people lose personal power is by giving it away. For instance, Cheryl Grace already had all the power and prestige she needed to keep succeeding at Nielsen. Anyone with business sense would have promoted Cheryl Grace to CEO. Her new CEO was just a corporate placeholder who was accustomed to benefitting from white, male privilege, and the corporation allowed this less forward-thinking white male to squash her vision and tried to take away all that she had earned for herself and for Nielsen. Luckily, Grace has fight, and she knows that if and when she leaves, she takes her talent with her. Ultimately, it's the corporation that loses out.

Young Black executives can follow her lead and fight toe-to-toe to the end without the worry of losing every inch they gain. Talent and intelligence are commodities that are highly sought after on the open market. No corporation has the right or the power to strip Black executives of those assets in the name of loyalty.

Jim Glover, founder, President, Creative Director/Writer of MultiCultural Creative Consultants (MCC), is another example of a self-made Black executive who faced white traditionalist opposition head on. He is well-known for a successful ad campaign that introduced McDonald's breakfasts to the masses, and for how he gracefully side-stepped racism in the workplace. Born and raised in Brooklyn, New York, Glover was a militant Black man and devout Muslim, fighting to win in the advertising industry in the late 1970s. Glover would only let racist jabs slide a few times before chin-checking white coworkers with jabs that stunned and stung their fragile egos.

Glover recalls a battle of wits with a German executive at Needham, Harper, and Steers, an ad agency in Chicago. The German executive would regularly make poorly veiled, derisive comments about Glover's Blackness. Glover says that he let it slide until one day, the man was bold enough to speak directly to him about taunting him. He looked at Glover and said, "I guess you're wondering why I always mess with you, huh, Jim?"

"I figure it's because you feel so bad about yourself," Glover replied.

The racist's face became beet red with embarrassment and anger, because deep down he knew Glover was right. Glover knew the man, not just a white man, but a European man, was fearful of a Black man, even though he knew that man was no match for his wits. Glover carefully put him in his place without giving up his own position of strength. The German executive could do nothing but laugh uncomfortably as he tried to save face, "Maybe you're right about that."

After the exchange, the German executive never gave Glover any trouble, setting a precedent which the other white executives followed. Glover admits now that he was often intimidated by the "white world" of business, and sometimes made silent agreements, yet he notes something every Black executive should take to heart: when he stood up, the enemy sat down.

Glover also kept racist white executives at bay by hanging posters of Black people being horrifically lynched and burned. He also hung a poster of an enslaved Black man. In the years to come, Glover rose in the ranks of various agencies. Though, he never removed his slave poster so that racists never forgot who he was, he admits he sometimes worried about being labeled a troublemaker—

code for a free-thinking Black man or woman who pushed for inclusion. Nevertheless, his career flourished.

Early in his career, Glover made up his mind to avoid creating the bland, almost corny advertising tactics that his white colleagues tapped into, like imitating jingles from the 1940s. Glover felt this approach was inauthentic, not only for him as a Black man, but for anybody. At the time, many ad agencies generated insincere content that was devoid of emotion. However, when McDonald's became a client of Needham, Harper, and Steers, Glover was assigned to write a commercial for the fast-food giant based on his musical background. His white colleagues were pleased when Glover recruited Woodstock legend, Ritchie Havens—not because he was Ritchie Havens, but because he was cheaper than Ray Charles. Haven's performance led to one of the most lucrative years in agency's history. The 1980 McDonald's ad with Ritchie Haven won Glover awards for years to come as he continued his work, recruiting more and more Black talent including world-renown artist Luther Vandross. Deep down, Glover felt vindicated—he was making money and winning awards. Moreover, he felt he was "sticking it to the man," while remaining authentic to himself and the Black community.

Years passed and Glover realized it didn't matter how much money he made for the agency, he just needed to leave. He found another agency, Leo Burnett in Chicago, which was far more comfortable financially if not psychologically. Regardless, he knew he would be better paid and that Leo Burnett would allow him to improve his craft. As soon as he received the offer from Leo Burnett, he knew he would take it, but out of business etiquette, he offered Needham, Harper, and Steers a chance to match the Leo Burnett offer. Glover wrote the offer on an envelope and handed it an administrative assistant to hand it to the head executives. However, the administrative assistant was nosy and vindictive. She opened the envelope and saw the offer then told everyone at the agency. This incited more battles with his colleagues. Not one of them felt he deserved such an offer, and they proceeded to harass and taunt him. Glover noted how it took a toll on him, but he was strong and not swayed by hate.

Glover left with his dignity, experience, awards, and few regrets. At Leo Burnett, Glover became the man with the Midas touch. Though there were still racists in his midst, they mostly kept their mouths shut. Glover only heard how they really felt about him through hearsay. But the racially fueled negativity was evident when Glover struggled to leap from Associate Creative Director to Creative Director. Nonetheless, Glover overcame many battles and, in many ways, shaped ad marketing in America and abroad for decades to come. He did it by learning to maneuver like a skilled boxer, never overexerting himself and hitting with precision and power.

In a 2021 podcast, Teddy Atlas, world-renown trainer and commentator, presented a number of strategies used by skilled boxers and pitfalls they should avoid. These same principles apply to how Black executives should fight for senior executive/C-suite level positions. An effective boxer gains momentum from his or her stance, drawing power from the floor then through the waist and hips, and translates that power into brute force that emanates through the shoulders, arms, and fists in solid punches. The Black executive must take a stance and firmly plant his or her feet, so he or she will be ready to explode with patience and precision.

Winning as a boxer is not about throwing explosive punches all the time. Power punches can miss or be interrupted with a quick counterpunch. Instead, it's about applying enough power and pressure to shake the opponent enough for him or her to fear the impact and shrink into don't-hit-me punch defenses. For Black executives doing battle in board rooms, being explosive or expressing their opinions in an overly provocative or defensive manner is the kiss of death. Many fail to consider this, and later, find that white executives have them trapped on the ropes or in the corner. A better way is to use an opponent's strength against them.

For instance, imagine that white executives are floating the idea of increasing the perceived value of the company brand simply by raising prices on current products or services to create a sense of exclusivity. While this is a common approach, the Black executive may realize that if there is no new offer per membership package, there will be a loss of membership regardless. white executives may reject the Black executive's arguments as a distraction or simply want to undermine it to help push their own ideas through. How the Black executive reacts to this push-back can be the difference between gaining full support or receiving patronizing comments that suggest the Black executive simply doesn't get it.

When the Black executive draws power from the floor, his or her own foundation of experience and knowledge, and stands firm, the result is more likely to be positive. The key is to present an alternative plan, backed by facts and statistics, that can still expand membership but not at the expense of customer satisfaction. The Black executive in this scenario understands that the company needs to maintain loyalty to its customer base to retain them, but white executives may be insistent that they've solved the problem.

If the Black executive is adamant about his or her position, he or she must throw and land the vital body shot so hard it knocks the wind out of the white executive's self-serving plan. If the Black executive is focused and not defensive, that punch becomes a pitch and expands the features and amenities through mutually beneficial partnerships with other companies who share the same customer base. The partnering companies can pay a small fee for marketing products and services featured in each membership package. Packages range from bronze, silver, gold, to diamond membership. The Black executive provides a plan that is self-supporting and builds business relationships which offers customers more value in exchange for higher membership costs.

Hitting back at a bad idea with a demonstrably better one, is like meeting a jab with a body shot. The Black executive will take that round.

A skilled boxer realizes that fighting with precision requires patience and timing. Timing is everything. Rushing to action indicates fear or not thinking, simply fighting off emotion and reacting.

The proactive fighter understands how foreseeing and matching the opponent's punches leads to an eventual win (Atlas, 2021). Atlas stresses that a thinking boxer is a calm one. Much like the boxer, the Black entrepreneur must always remain focused. One can't focus on the opponent in front of them by allowing a rush of unrelated thoughts and worries to enter his or her mind. Therefore, the thinking executive must also remain calm and not become emotional. The battle may be intense, but the Black executive must engage the opposition with level-headedness.

Unfortunately, Black men and especially Black women face the stereotype that they are irrational or emotional and may explode when opposed by white people. When white executives act in such ways, they are cheered on as passionate and assertive. The same cannot be said of Black executives. Corporate leaders often paint Black assertiveness as a sign that they are emotionally unbalanced and psychologically maladjusted. Black executives must remain calm to prevent such stereotypes from taking them off their game.

Staying calm during a heated exchange allows the Black executive to study the opposition in real time and think clearly in all situations. Once the Black executive notes patterns in the opponent's argument, say repeating a point that has already been clarified or consistently repeating falsehoods, then boom, the Black executive points out the fallacy and uses the white executive's flawed perspective to quell the argument altogether. Patience allows room for listening. This allows one to comprehensively assess an opponent's argument while dissecting it to reveal its internal contradictions. This is how the Black executive must weaken the opposing argument. This is the same technique used by boxers to win against worthy opponents in the ring. Patience on the part of one boxer creates the time and space for the opponent to wear out until—BOOM! – the boxer sees an opening and throws a hard left or right to the head, chest, or gut.

With calm precision, quick thinking, and responsive reaction, a boxer can deliver punches that land with a plan. The odds are in favor of Black executives if they allow the opponent to act unconsciously and use outdated or flawed thinking in their favor. Victory relies on giving the opposition room to make mistakes.

When Black executives present solutions that benefit the company as whole, support for Black executive strategies and insights increase despite racially fueled opposition. When white opponents attempt to refute a solid plan but can't produce a comparable alternative, their objections become moot and fall silent. That's when the Black executive, like the boxer, has landed a fatal blow, beating the opponent to the punch. As Teddy Atlas says, "Never let the opponent settle; rather, change the rhythm and flow of the fight to throw the opponent off" (Atlas, 2021).

On the flip side, Black executives, like boxers, must be careful not to wear themselves out on defense, because they will be led into the same trap. Instead, if the opponent is trying to wear them out, the Black executive can pretend to retreat, giving the enemy a false sense that they are growing tired of the fight. Once the opposition thinks they see their opening, the Black executive must be ready to throw the knockout punch. This is a rope-a-dope, and it is as effective in the corporate setting as it is in the ring. But Black executives must be cautious that they are not the dope in this scenario.

We often see the rope-a-dope used by white "Karens," or white women who harass Black and Brown men and women then shift from an accusatory tone to a tone of victimization. White men in a position of authority are always on the ready to defend a poor, defenseless white woman against an aggressive Brown or Black person, even if that person did not start the fight. White women know this, and they use it to their advantage. This scenario plays out in board rooms throughout America, so Black executives must use caution when being drawn into a battle so that they don't lose on a technicality.

Like boxers, Black executives must also consider range, his or her ability to throw a powerful punch, and the opponent's ability to throw punches in return. Blacks must know how far to take the argument or how far the opponent is willing to go to press an issue. Not understanding one's own range can lead Black executives to overextend themselves when they are throwing a punch, and that punch will either not land or land too softly to have the intended effect. Likewise, not understanding an opponent's range can expose vulnerabilities and is a one-way ticket to being knocked out or critically injured. Knowing one's range is a means to anticipate the return of fire from the opponent which demands adjustment, movement, and recovery to counter the opponent's tactic (Atlas, 2021).

In a fight, too many boxers perform for the crowd. They act as showmen versus strategists. Throwing a series of punches is ineffective, and they are easily thwarted. Boxers and Black executives never win by throwing the most punches. They win by throwing punches that land and only punches with power behind them are effective. Whoever lands the cleanest punch, lands the meanest punch. Those punches win (Atlas, 2021).

There are three areas of the body that are worth focusing on when throwing a punch: the head, the chest, the gut. A fighter can't perform if he or she can't breathe, so the chest is the most prized target. Hit an opponent in the face or side of the head, you take away his or her sight, hearing, or sense of balance. Hit an opponent in the gut, and a boxer can disable an opponent by weakening his or her core and/or ability to stand. A boxer can't continue to fight with effective power and precision when they have sustained a blow to one of these areas.

For Black executives, the head represents an opponent's thought patterns and use of logic. The chest represents the fervor with which an opponent enters a debate or discussion. The gut represents the core, the source from which all strength and drive is centered. Likewise, Black executives must defend their own heads, chests, and guts while inflicting injury on the opponent's vital areas to win the fight.

The chest can be protected by switching up lead hands and stances to keep a boxer from exposing themselves. Body shots, shots made straight to the gut, can sap an opponent's energy and limit their movements, causing them to think, "I might get hit again if I go here or there." Thus, the opponent begins to suffer from self-doubt and hold back. The more the opponent holds back, the more opportunity there is for a boxer to close in for the win.

When arguing before the administration, Black executives should allow room for white colleagues to exhaust themselves by building weak cases, raising invalid objections, or leading with hidden agendas. The Black executive doesn't have to do anything but give them enough rope to hang themselves. Allowing white executives to make specious or reactive arguments enables Black executives to expose them for their lack of clarity, discipline, or insight. It also exposes reactive, white-is-right stances as a liability to the company. This approach leads white executives to sit down, shut up, and move out of the way so Black leadership can do the real work of advancing the company.

According to a 2020 study by McKinney & Company, African Americans continue to be underrepresented in significantly higher paying fields, such as information technology, professional services, and financial departments. Consideration of higher paying fields and low diversity draws attention to symbiotic relationships between affluence and race reflected in continued disenfranchisement of African Americans in the private sector (Hancock et al., 2021).

African Americans not only remain underrepresented but underpaid in comparison to Caucasian contemporaries in the same positions (Hancock et al., 2021). African American men make 13% less than white men and 28% less than Asian men in private sector positions. Moreover, Black women make up only 2.7% of high-paying jobs in the private sector. Shockingly, Black women make 37% less than white men and 20% less than Black men while representing just over 6% of the private-sector workforce population (Miller, 2020).

Up-and-coming Black professionals that have their eyes on the prize of high-paying, executive positions, have a lot farther to go than their white counterparts. Forty-three percent of Black professionals initially make less than $30,000 per year. In the last 30 years, the fields in which Black professionals have significantly excelled are healthcare, retail, and accommodation/food services. Currently, 45% of the Black professional workforce occupies these fields, yet they still struggle to move beyond managerial positions into executive and administrative positions. Essentially, Black professionals are forced to remain in service roles versus leading in operations, financial management, or administration within the three frontline industries (Hancock et al., 2021).

Black professionals make up just 7% of private sector management and 4% of senior management and executive positions combined. Black professionals represent less than 10% of the workforce in the fast-growing cities in America (Hancock et al., 2021). Moreover, entry-level positions can be a revolving door for many Black professionals with no advancement in sight due to a resistance to promotion and a cycle of unilateral transfers, or movement from department to department. Transfers within a company ensure that Blacks move sideways and never up. Essentially, Blacks are treated as stand-ins or place fillers with no real prestige or expectation that they will become star fighters. Being held down in this way often leads Black professionals to leave and consider entrepreneurships.

A lack of support and the notion that Black professionals are corporate pawns maintains a trust deficit that has existed between Black professionals and corporate America since the 1970's. Integration never meant incorporation. The reality is that Blacks are given an equal opportunity to work but not to manage or lead. A lack of mentorship and allyship within predominantly white-led companies isolates and marginalizes Black professionals. Most Black professionals feel they are unlikely to receive support, even when they present plans of action to further their careers. Conversely, white contemporaries regularly receive inside assistance through direct administrative support. Such support pipelines push white professionals—and often Asian-Americans—to the forefront.

According to McKinsey & Company, with the current rate of arrested development, it will take another 100 years for Black professionals to reach talent parity, equal pay, and leadership prevalence equal to white professionals (Hancock et al., 2021). Within 20 years—by 2040—the racial shift in population will lean more toward Latino and African Americans due to lower birth rates among whites; yet Black people may have to wait another 80 years after American demographics shift to experience job equality. This is clearly unacceptable, but if Black want to shorten the timeline, they must be prepared to go toe-to-toe with no mercy.

Nevertheless, past progress is evident. Through the concerted efforts of non-Black allies and companies seeking to revise their organizational culture in response to public pressure, Black professionals are excelling in transportation. But to change this dynamic in all sectors across the board, Blacks must build and maintain stronger bridges between service positions, management positions, and senior level positions.

According to a 2020 study conducted by McKinsey & Company, less than 25% of Black professionals feel they receive support, yet nearly one-third of white professionals believe that they have been given a leg up. The more that Black executives demand inclusion and seek resources that promote significant inclusion, the more Black leadership will be incorporated. At present, this can only be accomplished through "toe-to-toe" combat.

Fighting demands dedication, training to win, performing to win, and finishing the fight. Continuing to fight against white-is-right thinking can feel futile, but history has shown that when blatant racists and sexists openly belittle, berate, and deny Black people their seat at the table, Black professionals can win by taking a firm stand. Toe-to-toe exchanges are more difficult, because for every punch traded, Black executives must expose themselves to potential injury. To survive this, they must fight with as much passion as skill. Veteran boxers anticipate injury. The boxer knows how to roll with the punches versus just taking a punch. When the skilled boxer is hit, he or she homes in on the opponent's exposed weakness and fires back with a concrete counterpunch. It is common to see skilled boxers leave a ring bloodied and beaten. Fighters are trained to overcome such injuries and keep fighting. Black professionals must do the same, because when they allow injuries to distract them from their fight for victory, they have already lost.

Both Muhammad Ali and Mike Tyson used forms of psychological warfare to win fights before any punches were ever thrown. The genius of both Ali and Tyson wasn't brute strength or skill, both got tagged several times and physically suffered pain. Both broke down their opponents through the use of old-fashioned intimidation. They made their opponents believe they couldn't win. Black executives must employ similar tactics. In the corporate setting, one can't use rudeness or aggression to achieve this goal without falling victim to cultural stereotypes, but they can enter the ring with the impenetrable certainty that they will win. Confidence is often more powerful than anger, and confidence backed by skill can be impossible to defeat.

The goal for Black executives should be to move from dancing around an argument to standing flatfooted and steadfastly fighting for what they believe in. A Black executive must move like a boxer and adjust to attacks and counterattacks by noting the opponent's fighting style. They can learn a lot from the four main types of boxers: swarmer's, out-boxers, sluggers, and boxer-punchers. The swarmer throws up a series of punches hoping they will land one while simultaneously attempting to crowd the opponent. In many ways, this style is like the don't-hit-me-punch style in which a boxer has no strength or strategy and simply wants to get through the round.

The out-boxer seeks to outscore and mark the opponent. In a heated discussion, white executives feel confident they can out-box Black executives by undercutting the validity of their opinions using racial stereotyping and gaslighting. Black executives often feel that they can do nothing but defend themselves, but this approach quickly them out and highlights the weaknesses in their resolve. Black executives should instead skillfully return attacks and shift the balance to put white leaders on the defensive. If they do not, they face certain defeat.

The slugger is similar to the swarmer, but slower and more precise. In the corporate environment, a slugger will throw out heavy, hard-hitting points followed by complex, longwinded explanations intended to validate it. Black executives can defeat this approach by throwing equally heavy punches targeted to areas where his or her opponent shows weakness. As previously discussed, the three points of weakness are the head, chest, and gut. No boxer can protect all three at the same time, and no boxer is strong in all three areas. White executives reveal their weakness when hit, holding one hand back to defend the area while throwing blows with the other. When the Black slugger identifies areas of weakness, he or she must work those areas relentlessly to handicap the opponent and put the argument to bed. When white executives respond by overexplaining, the Black executive knows this is a sensitive area and thus can use that weakness to his or her advantage.

The last fighting approach is the boxer-puncher style. Boxer-punchers are masterful at close-range exchanges in which the trading of blows is heavy, quick, and snappy. The only way to counter the speed, rhythm, and strength of such an attack is to recover quickly and maintain a mobile defense that has the fluidity of water but the resistance of ice. In a verbal exchange, white executives who employ the boxer-puncher style may throw out random points that border on insult, seeking to incite some form of emotional response from the Black executive. When Blacks respond emotionally, they too expose potential vulnerabilities that can easily be exploited. The best example of this style is that of Donald Trump taking on Hillary Clinton in the 2016 Presidential Debate. Clinton attempted to exchange blow for blow with Trump, but her weakness was quickly revealed, for Trump did not adhere to the traditional debate structure. Rather, he sat back and watched her try to defeat him through long explanations, then awkward responses, then no responses, which made Donald Trump appear as if he had overwhelmed Clinton. Of course, we know that Clinton was more prepared to answer tough debate questions, but perception is everything. This style of attack won over the audience and positioned Trump as the better fighter.

In the first 2020 Presidential Debate between Joe Biden and Donald Trump, Trump tried to employ this approach again, but he had met his match. Joe Biden's unbothered responses deflated the heft of Trump's pointless attacks and left-field utterances and shined a light on the fact that Trump was the undisciplined, unskilled fighter in the ring. Joe Biden didn't let Trump distract him and get a rise out of him. This only made Trump all the more frustrated and erratic. The public saw Donald Trump as unstable. He was outboxed. At one point, Trump began arguing with the moderator, and Joe Biden brought attention to this outlandish behavior by saying, "Will you shut up, man??" Trump actually shut up for a moment. He had winded himself like a two-year-old throwing a tantrum. Biden was able to finish his point, and took charge of the debate, which he won without breaking a sweat. Black executives that are preparing to go toe-to-toe against a white-is-right corporation can emulate Biden's style by grounding themselves in their principles, believing in their own ideas, and never allowing the shady techniques of their opponents shake their stance.

WISDOM TO APPLY IN
THE CORPORATE RING:

• Some Black executives are so fearful of losing what little they've been given by white-led corporations, they pull punches, fail to cover themselves, or react in an unseemly manner out of weakness rather than strength. Such reactions give corporations control over the flow of the fight, and when it eventually wears down the boxer, leaders are free to change up their fighting style and go for the knockout.

• Black executives have unique talents and strengths that corporations need. That is why they were hired. They need to realize that they do not owe blind loyalty or a willingness to play second fiddle to whites in order to maintain the respect of their peers. Instead, they gain respect by not folding to the powers that be and not accepting veiled threats as inevitable job loss.

• An effective boxer gains momentum from his or her stance, drawing power from the floor then through the waist and hips, and translates that power into brute force that emanates through the shoulders, arms, and fists in solid punches. The Black executive must take a stance and firmly plant his or her feet, so he or she will be ready to explode with patience and precision.

- If the Black executive is adamant about his or her position, he or she must throw and land the vital body shot so hard it knocks the wind out of the white executive's self-serving plan. If the Black executive is focused and not defensive, that punch becomes a pitch and expands the features and amenities through mutually beneficial partnerships with other companies who share the same customer base.

Fighting demands dedication, training to win, performing to win, and finishing the fight. Continuing to fight against white-is-right thinking can feel futile, but history has shown that when blatant racists and sexists openly belittle, berate, and deny Black people their seat at the table, Black professionals can win by taking a firm stand.

BOXING STRATEGY

TRUST YOUR CORNER TEAM

Make sure you have people in your corner that understand your fighting style and the fighting style of your opponent. When it's time to throw in the towel, your cornermen should tell you before you fall victim to a career-ending blow. When they throw in the towel on your behalf, think hard before getting back in the fight.

Throwing in
THE TOWEL

Professional boxers don't fight alone. They have cornermen (or women) who help them prepare for fights, bring them water and ice packs, or tape them up between rounds. Those people are also ready to throw in the towel if it looks as though their fighter is taking a career-ending beating.

Many people don't realize that the phrase "throwing in the towel" is a physical act, but, yes, it actually involves throwing a white towel into the ring to signal to the referee that the fight should end. Of course, the referee is the only one who can call a fight, so the simple toss of a towel isn't considered an official acknowledgement of defeat. Still, it happens.

In corporate America, many Black executives don't have cornermen looking out for their best interests. When they throw in the towel, they throw it in alone, and often too late to prevent long-term damage to their careers. But that is not what's on a Black executive's mind when it happens. There simply comes a point when Black executives are so worn down from workplace discrimination that they no longer have the will to fight back.

The act of throwing in the towel is completely understandable. Human beings aren't built to sustain the amount of stress and degradation that many Blacks do day after day. It's a slow and methodical technical fight designed to wear Blacks down. But Black executives must realize they cannot give up, because the minute they do could be the very minute their career is about to turn a corner, and they will have given away their dreams to people who won't think twice about them when they are gone.

It's hard to imagine in the moment, because burn out and despair can creep in slowly and build over time. It's a three-part process of giving in, giving out, and giving up. We give in when we know that what we acquiesce to will cause discomfort, but we find the goal or reward worth the pain. In corporate America, Black executives already understand that they may be treated as a Black mascot, a liaison to handle Black employees, or for use as a corporate image meant to show diversity. We give in by allowing such treatment by agreeing to take on roles that propagate Eurocentric views of African Americans while excluding our own values, needs, and goals. When Black executives allow themselves to succumb, submit, and be subjugated to these stereotypes, they are accepting self-sanctioned slavery.

Corporate slavery is not far from actual slavery in which Blacks were manipulated into accepting their plight. Many accepted slavery out of fear, others for rewards from slave owners, and later racist leaders under Jim Crow. Today's racial exclusionists still advocate for the use of Black labor yet limit the influence, development, and independence of the Black workforce. This specifically undermines African American interests in C-suite level leadership.

By giving in, Black executives begin to carry out their assignments as programmed. At first, they take action creatively and compassionately. They make sure that they not only do as assigned, and they seek the validation of their supervisor. This leads to accepting their indoctrination and putting a greater value on compliance rather than respect for oneself. This can lead to depression, psychological issues, or even suicidal thoughts. It is a downhill spiral from the initial feeling of inauthenticity.

Many Black executives make the conscious decision not to be self-destructive, to rediscover their self-worth beyond their job, position, or a potential promotion. At that point, they assert themselves to regain a deeper sense of self-actualization that leads to either leaving and becoming an entrepreneur, or working for a predominantly Black organization, or they stay. Some stay and stay strong. But the physical and emotional wear and tear leads to burnout even among the best of workers. Few will be successful and achieve the goal of attaining an executive, senior level, or C-suite position. Many give out.

Giving out is when the mind and body break. It is complete burnout, which usually results in disdain for corporate America among Black executives. This disdain marks the beginning of the end for most Black executives. They ask themselves why they bought into the "bs" – biased scenarios. They realize their true reasoning for initially giving in and discover that they were never going to change the system from the inside or be a pioneer. Many realize that their greed and self-centered approaches have led them to allow racist behaviors and biased situations to progress. Once it all begins to exceed the Black executive's capabilities, tolerance, and patience, it's too late. They are caught up and slowly giving out. Morale drops. There is no connection to the work. There is no sense of redeeming oneself by attacking what's wrong within the overall administration and executive decisions impact the very goals, structure, and function of the organizational culture, corporate image, and direction of the company itself.

Worn to the core, Black executives struggle through assignments. Their accuracy and timeliness suffer due to psycho-emotional challenges, which leads to attacks on their performance by the same white executives who demand that Black executives do their bidding accordingly or face removal of support within a given position. Once this happens, the Black executive, who is now on his or her last proverbial leg, either leaves or still tries to hang in there, before he or she is reprimanded, warned, placed on an action plan, placed in a retraining program, or terminated. If, he or she can't carry out the "executive plan" accordingly, the Black executive will be terminated, approached with a severance package, demoted, or transferred.

The transfer often appears harmless and benign, a way for the Black executive to expand his or her resume to better serve the company or if not one company, or the industry itself. However, transfers disrupt consistent performance and the ability to build a stable administrative history. Black executives can feel like bologna at the end of their careers—processed meat, stripped of authenticity and pumped full of artificial flavors and preservatives (i.e. anti-Black employee perspectives and actions that serve racist agendas). Once the Black executive gives up, it's over. He or she may go into business for themselves or work in Black-owned businesses or other businesses of color that cater to African American interests and needs. Or a Black executive will simply leave the world of business and leave their dreams behind.

The attrition rate of Black executives from corporate America is greater than the number of African Americans who are accepted into the senior executive pipeline. This needs to stop. Black executives must resist leaving a company due to this racialized, corporate burnout. Black executives, please do not give up! The battle is not at the beginning at all. Rather, we are surely in the middle of the melee, and we will win the war in the end.

Following recent events in which Trumpublican terrorists screamed their verses of extremism and stormed into the U.S.

Capitol building on January 6, 2021, the remaining hundreds of thousands of white Americans sat back in shock, wondering what to do next. Many, from our neighbors to political leaders to business leaders, were shocked to learn that America has always been dysfunctional and not the functional society in which it is portrayed. America is not safe for all people. It is obvious that racist notions of government have provided white people with white privilege long before 1776, but on the 6th of January, many factions of conservative right politicians and pundits saw for themselves how white privilege can be destructive for all who feed into it and support it for the purpose of undermining the pluralistic network of people who seek authentic, inclusive incorporation of all people in American society, specifically in the American economy.

Like a boxer, the Black executive is often caught between utter defeat, severe injury, or embarrassment to the point where it appears that he or she can't continue. He or she may look to the corner for cues. But even when a fighter feels empowered and believes he or she can overcome the attacks, regain footing, and keep fighting, it often seems wiser to give up rather than suffering serious injury, making it impossible to compete in future contests. Continuing to fight can result in mental and physical harm or even, unfortunately, death. Executives look to their trainers as protectors who will be ready to call it off to save the fighter and mitigate injury beyond defeat.

The fighter doesn't have to agree with the trainer. Many times, he or she will disagree, but the trainer will throw in the towel when the fighter does not submit to the fact that he or she is losing. They know when it's time to accept a necessary loss to allow healing, growth, and the eventual return to the ring to fight another day. Yet, so many Black executives continue to fight on, refusing to accept defeat, which is when they fall and risk losing everything.

Most Black executives must be their own trainers, their own protection from a devastating defeat. Throwing in the towel for oneself is hard, especially when an individual is suffering from exhaustion, depression, and burnout, and looking back at their careers and personal lives as one big joke or a waste of time. This is sad on so many levels. Yet by giving up on one intense battle in the boardroom, a Black executive can potentially extend his or her time within a position. He or she must accept that doubling down on one bout could lead to a position-ending or even career-ending outcome.

Embracing the reality that defeat could lead to the end of a career is a good reason to throw in the towel, but one must know a comeback is possible, whether that means leaving a company, heading to another, transferring within a company, or seeking organizational checks and balances from factions of the company culture who can remedy micro-aggressive conflicts. These are strategies that will allow Black executives not to feel that they are not completely outmatched when opposing corporate forces with no resources to recover from a prolonged battle with racist, white traditionalists and complacent executives of color who claim to support them.

For many Black executives, clashes in the boardroom that are fueled by racism and racialized sexism are simply small skirmishes, battles that do not define the war. This war is one of will in the face of opposition to racist, sexist, classist beliefs by elitists who see themselves losing their grip on complete power. Every Black executive who stays in the game—despite the threat of losing themselves or placing themselves in potential psychological harm—stands as a pillar upon which a new foundation of Black, Afrocentric leadership can grow. Through these executives, businesses can proactively grow into more profitable, more ethical organizations. But they will still need to fight against predominantly white leadership that seeks to make trouble for Black executives that are unwilling to be indoctrinated into serving the good-ole-boy, business-as-usual power structure.

Black executives feel a sense of isolation that eventually takes its toll, leaving many to face uncertainty regarding how solid their footing is. Many Black executives feel that their experiences are solely defined by their race. Even among Black women dealing with white men and women, race is considered before gender, followed by any other demographic factors that biased, bigoted leadership see as outside of their values, focus, or understanding. One's race provides opportunity only to be indoctrinated into a racist system. Thus, many Black executives feel the initial honor of being a first or one of very few to attain the power—to be "the man or woman for the job."

Many think to themselves, "How can we change the system if we don't try to work within it first?" Very democratic, transformational, inspirational, and diplomatic, but realistically, there has to be a more complex approach to address the challenges facing Black executives daily, versus simplified, simpleminded platitudes that only serve as a hollow coping mechanisms for dealing with very real challenges to the sovereignty of Afrocentric authenticity, and integrity. Black executives have to remember not to be seduced into forfeiting their Blackness and ultimately whitewashing their perspectives and values.

Black executives try to hold on to perspectives and values, historically and culturally shared by African Americans. They are willing to accept the challenges that Black people face as consumers, employees, or executives. This is where many Black executives create their own disconnect and may feel burdened by being hired for an administrative position based on their race. Race limits them from certain positions, and they receive other positions for racially motivated reasons. Many Black executives carry the burden of feeling that their position is seen as an accomplishment for their people versus for themselves as professional individuals. This causes internal anger and resentment about not being seen for their own work. Black executives grow tired of hearing the age-old racist comment, "You're a credit to your race," which is actually a slight that stems from the racist white perspective, suggesting that accomplished Black people are an anomaly—advanced specimens among a socially, cognitively, and ethically-challenged race. Sounds a lot harsher than the words themselves, but not when you read between the lines.

The belief that accomplished Blacks are the exception and not the rule is propagated by patronizing racists and fake liberals who practice white patronage at the corporate level to feel better about themselves. Meanwhile, Black executives are left with a sense of being pulled in opposing directions and vacillate between being the "people's champ" and the "administration's chump." Because of this, Black executives experience debilitating diversity fatigue that arises when an individual executive knows he or she is only chosen to represent Black people or people of color. Individually, no one person knows every aspect of their entire racial/ethnic group, especially when that group represents a vast range of related cultures from various nations or an entire continent. Black executives should be tapped for insights into projects geared to assist African American consumers and communities, but at the same time, these same professionals can also assist non-Black populations based on their executive skills, insights, and experiences of being an all-American professional with a proud African ancestry (Roberts & Mayo, 2019).

Black executives face harsh challenges no different than front-liners of democracy who protest in the streets. Yet there is no Black Executives Matter equivalent to the Black Lives Matter movement. The development of such networks would enable the growth of Black leadership and solidify their influence in corporate

America, because when people are placed in a nurturing environment with resources, camaraderie, and a focus on innovation, influence leads to results. Results lead to growth.

For years, Black innovation and economic prowess led to the growth of white-led corporations, but now, it is time for conscious Black executives to invest in themselves and give corporations reasons to invest in Black leadership, such as greater financial gain founded on greater ethical and social solidarity. With support, Black leaders can thrive in a more equitable atmosphere where they can express Black executive authenticity without reprimand because they have social, legal, and occupational representation. Representation means that their interests matter as much as that of white executives, and thus retaliation that is racially rooted is nullified. The greater the support, the less likely Black executives are to face challenges that undermine their ascension to C-Suite-level positions where they can fight for that "championship belt."

Many Black executives feel less attached, less bound by the mission and values of their corporations than whites or Hispanics, due to a perceived and actual lack of inclusiveness. Black management, supervisors, and executives report that there is a seedy side of companies in which Black employees are still made to feel like they are "the help" versus being leaders of operations and drivers of progress within their companies. Black leaders are steeped in inhospitable environments created and maintained by so-called mainstream organizational administrations. The constant feeling of being the "other" or an "outsider" causes Black executives to consider throwing in the towel every day, but, somehow, many keep moving forward.

Despite decades' old research stating that inclusive, incorporating, pluralistic administrations yield far more profit and function with greater success than monolithic, Eurocentric organizations, corporate America has yet to do what they say and open the flood gates to the Black executive masses. Corporations toot their public service/ social advocacy horns and claim solidarity with Black America, but beyond words, the only solidarity these corporations have is based on Black dollars and the Black labor they exploit to make white administrators and company investors even richer.

A corporation's refusal to recruit, train, and place more African Americans in upper-level leadership positions, it usually results in high attrition rates among Black professionals, leading to greater losses in corporate earnings than previously understood by economists and social advocates alike. The loss of Black executive talent impacts earning capacity, organizational culture, commercial insight, and corporate innovation. When corporate America loses, Black entrepreneurs gain substantial Black but also non-Black clientele. Black businesses generate remarkable profits and create competition for white-led businesses. When African Americans build corporations, they give predominantly white-led corporations a run for their money, leading to competitive bids to buy, merge, or acquire shares. Buyouts, mergers, and acquisitions lead to eventual absorption of these Black-owned assets, and many Black members of the original entity are voted out, contractually forced out, or knee-capped with a role equal to a figurehead.

Black executives must be strong enough to consistently find internal and external supports to realize professional ascension. They need a culture that supports Black assertiveness and a means to present to non-Black employees and benefit from collaboration versus needless competition. When there is a clear, corporate message that employees' jobs and futures are safe, Blacks will be better able to collaborate, and companies will enjoy the benefits of teamwork versus internal squabbles that only lower morale and maintain a toxic, racialized, sexualized organizational culture. Black executives must know that they are not burdened by diversity but strengthened by it, so they can initiate and maintain control over various diversity and inclusion endeavors to spread and establish multicultural executive models throughout corporate American leadership.

It is the Black executive's responsibility to raise awareness and seek the support of allies among various demographics within the workforce. This strengthens social connections and creates a team-based atmosphere versus a competitive collection of factions divided by social ideologies centered on demographic differences. The archaic model of American business that excluded women of all colors and non-white men must now include them according to laws established some 50 years ago, such as Title VII of the 1964 Civil Rights Act, regarding employment discrimination, and Title IX of 1972 Education Amendments, regarding educational discrimination. However, translating those laws from ideological words and abstract edicts into actions and behaviors has proven difficult, except in instances of extreme chaos such as terrorist attacks or civil unrest.

Exclusive, Eurocentric, male-dominated administrators create a fractured workforce, but the very real losses to corporations may not always be apparent. But they will become more obvious when corporations lose to competitors who embrace pluralistic administration. These corporations that embrace pluralistic administration with a primary focus on African American leadership, who openly display their support and solidarity with the Black community, can influence firms they partner with in terms of how they address the needs of not only immediate market segments but the environments in which such populations live and work. This is where the Black executive becomes the true go-to person, but not solely to answer the question, "What do Black people think?" This question is equal to asking a white man or woman what every white person thinks. No, what Black executives possess is how to best address the needs, images, values, and perspectives of a spectrum of different African American consumers.

Black executives, in collaboration with conscious, white executives, need to encourage open conversations about race and gender in respect to current sociopolitical events and the toxic mentalities behind them regarding corporate America and the very streets of our nation. Corporations, institutions, and organizations must realize they cannot exist within a bubble that runs counter to the realities of the society around them. These business entities are part of the very societies they ignore. Those corporations that seek authenticity and fairness need to practice what they preach and prove that they are willing to take action to improve society beyond simply selling products and services. What is the benefit of turning

233

a profit when your customer base is alienated, or employees work in an adversarial atmosphere? The negative experiences non-white employees have with the police, the justice system, school administrations, housing and banking authorities are real. Until corporations make an effort to improve employees' lives beyond simply giving them a job, American corporations will never reap the benefits of equality.

Organizations that do more than talk about the challenges Black people face, and instead, take part in providing solutions that address nutrition, training and education, and financial stability can pipeline economically challenged Black children from students to professionals to corporate executives. Such programs should begin as early as middle school and continue through college matriculation, graduation, recruitment, and beyond the point of hire. The consistent support that many white graduates/employees enjoy keeps them involved in organizations as "team members." This dynamic needs to be fully extended to African American employees equally, regardless of their rank or position. Yet it is the responsibility of Black executives and employees alike to actively monitor, assess, and revise such assistance programs within American corporations.

Complaining about how current business is, but not taking a proactive role to change it, is like throwing in the towel but still trying to swing at the opposition. Doing so is all for show and not scoring points. The boxer has officially conceded.

Organizations are reflections of their communities as well as influencers of everyday society. Marvel Comics and DC Comics have made an effort to create strong Black superhero movies and TV shows and to promote Black leadership in their given "universes" as a norm. Think Samuel L. Jackson as Nick Fury (Marvel), Chadwick Boseman as King T'Challa the Black Panther (Marvel), Jordan Calloway as Painkiller (DC), or Cress Williams as Black Lightning (DC). Racism, sexism, and other forms of bias are addressed in the storylines. Stan Lee originally created the Mutants as representations of Black people with Professor X as a representation of Dr. King and Magneto as a representation of Malcolm X. Both leaders fought for the freedom of Mutantkind, but the storyline has maintained the conflict between peaceful integration versus revolutionary takeover conflict for nearly 60 years.

The success of *Black Panther* lies in its representation of the values and visions of Black people, people of African descent, remaining autonomous yet having the ability to work together with those who differ. This ideology is very American. This concept of different people coming together to battle a common enemy works in the world of fantasy and makes fans smile and pay lots of money. When we think of young, white children running around in Black Panther masks, we see an America that is accepting and inclusive, but, at its core, it is still marketing that leads to more money for companies. However, these commercial efforts still result in a psychosocial change that proactively impacts society.

Black children and their families experience a sense of pride from the narrative of Black Panther and his character's ability to command Africans, Caucasians, and African American characters alike. Children growing up in the age of this celebrated Black superhero will grow into adults of the 2030s and 2040s. They will lead society. This is not to say that because a white child in Boise, Idaho saw and loved *Black Panther* as a child, he or she won't still grow up and share the same sentiments as some QANON conspiracy theorists, but it's less likely if that child is consistently exposed to and interacts with positive representations of Black people and their perspectives. The Black child who feels pride based on the *Black Panther* phenomenon may not grow up to run for public office or be the CEO of an organization, but the impact on his or her sense of self-worth is influenced by how corporate America—this includes American multimedia companies—portrays people based on the continuous reshaping of traditional biased perspectives.

The same proactive psychological and sociological outcomes can happen in organizations that promote positive Black images and Black leadership. Not even Marvel or DC have showcased Black talent publicly at such levels, but neither of these organizations have received the backlash that related organizations such as Disney (who owns Marvel) have received for failure to promote more proactive Black images, and above all, to showcase Black leadership in real time. That is where the real story lies and where the real Black superheroes need to be seen. Black executives need to force conversations concerning race. True, they face being fired, demoted, or simply censured or ignored, but that leads to them leaving and taking success elsewhere. Nevertheless, they will not be broken. They will not give in, give out, or give up.

The challenge for many Black executives is white discomfort with diversity and inclusion conversations, because, unfortunately, many white executives feel white guilt, and when they are forced to face their white privilege and self-assess their own level of bias along racial and racialized gender lines, they are uncomfortable. White guilt and white privilege are natural results of white patriarchy. This is racism in its underlying form. This is where institutional racism and overt racism support each other, and it takes place every day in every boardroom across America based on the fear that many white people and white executives have regarding power wielded by Black people. The primary fear is that Black leadership will detract from white capabilities, values, and resources. Fear distorts reality. This is the same fear spewed by Trump which led to insurrection.

Does the U.S. want to see an underlying response of explosive racism within corporate America similar to the Trump Insurrection from the like-minded, but simpleminded supporters of monolithic domination of white rule in every aspect of society? The answer lies in the actions corporations take from the date of the Insurrection moving forward. What they have done, attempted to do, or claim they will do is all balderdash at this point, but it is clear that Black executives must know that the urgency for corporations to maintain customer bases—and thus profits—is at hand. It is time that Black executives show these corporations the ethical reasons they need to grow and change their corporate credo and related practices. These corporations need to revise their missions and visions to reflect the morals and values of Black leadership for each brand's given organizational culture. Once those cultures reflect positive Black influence, then the solidarity of such corporations will be authentic. From that authenticity, profits will grow, but this will be secondary to the primary focus of providing quality products and services that reflect the values and perspectives defined by each market segment autonomously and on their terms, not those who are external of the given market segment's demographic. Moreover, as corporations make Black leadership a norm within corporate America, the Black executive population in C-suite-level positions will skyrocket.

Any conversations that take place regarding these issues should make all parties feel comfortable about speaking and sharing. Discomfort on the part of whites is like the discomfort of demons in the presence of a crucifix. The racist notions, the demons, that some white executives refuse to let go of represent a choice. Black executives also have a choice, continue the fight or simply throw in the towel. Despite the actions of such die-hard racists, Black executives can seek alliances with white executives and other members of administration who are compassionate and collaborative with a vision to meet benchmarks that ensure corporate growth by addressing the corporation not as a business but as a workforce of autonomous peoples working together. This pluralistic approach is founded upon the value of incorporating diversity in all aspects of organizations, which leads to greater performance and expansion and shows society a means of improving functionality. Improving corporate functionality from a pluralistic approach means embracing diversity within leadership and administration.

To slow and eventually stop Black executives from throwing in the towel, Black executive advocacy committees need to seek internal resources such as conscious white team members who can begin the conversation about race as a means to address their organization's structure and future. This reflects greater solidarity to demarginalize and fully-integrate the workforce through support for leadership that reflects key segments of the target market, communities across the country, and the values of those communities as they define them for themselves. Prominent leaders such as Kaiser Permanente's Bernard Tyson, AT&T's Randall Stephenson, and Morgan Stanley's global head of D&I, Susan Reid have begun a movement, a process of using culturally relevant conversations and thinktanks to address racial learning and bring employee groups together with awareness of their positions and views regarding inclusiveness and empowerment within their organizations and their communities (Roberts & Mayo, 2019).

What Black executives must prepare for and mitigate at

all costs is diversity and inclusion programs that slowly collapse under the mismanagement of so-called white allies and supporters who only present an alternative to exclusion and expulsion of Black leadership by offering to manage Blackness. The concept of managing Blackness has a loaded meaning as if handling people who are uncontrollable, out of order, or simply need to be taken care of. Managing Blackness is a matter of extracting what is considered universally valuable to the overall population of stakeholders. This is only doubletalk for whitewashing various aspects of sensitivities that are important to a variety of Black people. These aspects must be served with Black authenticity defined autonomously by Afrocentric values.

Through Black authenticity in executive leadership, corporate America can approach market segments with authenticity regarding marketing, outreach, utilizing feedback, design, and progress. It's the same with leaders who are white. They may not represent all white perspectives alone, yet they provide applicable insights regarding related demographics within their overall target market population. However, a model that assumes there are conscious white leaders who will somehow caretake, mentor, and sponsor Black career and leadership development has been costly to Black executives since the 1970s. It never succeeded in any significant form. The fact is that Black leadership in major corporations has been reduced from miniscule to microscopic within the last 20 years. So, in that sense, Black executives have a grave amount of work ahead to maintain the little bit of C-suite ground they had and expand on the power Black people must have in the future.

Despite supporting studies, as well as obvious need to be inclusive and incorporative of Black people in administrations throughout corporate America, Black executives still face challenges to self-preservation being maintained and this is an immediate concern. Nevertheless, here is where numbers matter as a means of fortifying or increasing the strength and power among Black executives as teams, groups, and organizations within corporations. As a force, Black executives can organize and mobilize to provide legal, moral, educational, and financial support to enable greater Black progression in American business. Self-preservation is often a key area of focus among professionals because they felt threatened by the possibility of losing what they have. However, when they feel they are not alone, they are willing to fight harder for more. Black executives must stop the "me against the world" belief and seek to support each other, even if it means facing the loss of a job position at a specific company. With greater organizational support, the fear of losing ground will lessen. If it does not, companies will face greater litigation, bad press, and key market segments—not solely Black consumers but non-Black consumers that have solidarity with the Black community.

True, there are unscrupulous, backstabbing executives that are Black who are worse than any racist, white executive, and they would be terrible for a Black executive team, committee, or organization, however, for the most part, the threat would more than likely be from racists looking at any form of Black unity and power within their organization as a threat. It has always been a social nuance that whites who find Blacks congregating without white supervision or influence perceive them as a threat. Yet, when it comes to what threatens Black executive development, Black executives no different than Latino/Hispanic, Asian, or Jewish professionals, must form stronger sociocultural/ethnic networks to provide Black executives a safety net, resources, and choices to ensure their personal and professional stability within their career (Sisco, 2020).

The Black executive who does not give up must consider the rematch, the comeback. The Black executive knows that if he or she threw in the towel previously, that towel came with a string to snatch that rag off the ring floor faster than when Mike Tyson hit an opponent

243

and that opponent hit the floor. Black executives have to be strategic ninjas rather than strategic boxers. They have to have the agility of a martial artist with ninjitsu, kung fu, and Muay Thai skills.

The Black executives who understands the comeback also understands the value of time, patience, development, and the means to rebuild their images, supplies, networks, and means to return strong and confident in the boardroom, in the field, in operational assignments, or in strategy meetings without the handicap of past experiences hanging over them. This can take place in the same industry, same company, same department, or same team. Throwing in the towel in these scenarios is often easier than permanently giving up and leaving corporate America altogether. It can take place during a time when a Black executive decides to take a leave of absence, transfer, take a vacation, even quit (but with re-hirable status), and later they return.

Either way, staying in one's current company, moving to competitors, or even partnering with other companies can feel to a Black executive like being a fly simply going from one spider web to the other. But the Black executive who thinks like the boxer understands that they are gaining strategies based on past fights, correcting trajectory, power, balance, agility, speed, and means to surprise their opposition in order to maneuver into positions where access to power cannot be denied. Again, it is best for the Black executive to continuously understand and exercise what many white executives fear Black executives do most and make everything beyond any non-disclosure agreements public. They must make what is routine internal policy public such as the training of, treatment of, socialization of, and interaction with Black executives by predominantly white companies transparent.

New projects and developments along with their outcomes can benefit the Black executive not only in ways such as building a list of accomplishments in the name of the brand, but also when periods of strife, challenge, or even failure take place, Black executives can take the responsibility despite threats of termination and micro-aggressive harassment by white executives and redesign projects to be executed in a fashion that gains greater accomplishment. In that ideal sense, it is a win-win situation. By using public, media-based, sociopolitical, environmental, and above all commercial venues to display corporate actions, Black executives potentially could acquire even greater positions and influence in the majority of American corporations and their international franchises.

America is a culture built on peer pressure. When one company sees another taking part in sociopolitical, economic, or ecological practices that benefit that company's abilities to connect more with key market segments, corporations tend to move like trees—slowly leaning in the direction toward more light with roots stretching out deeper in the soil searching for more water and more resources, so to speak. Corporate behaviors that stress social advocacy followed by actions to ensure racial and gender-based equality support a multicultural customer base with pluralistic leadership incorporation. This is perfect for brands that cater to or seek to gain African American customers. However, the same needs to take place among businesses that may not have significant clientele of color but have African Americans throughout their workforce. Peer pressure doesn't seem to have the same effect on such businesses when they are still meeting their financial and productivity goals. Therefore, the means to pressure such companies lies not only in social advocacy groups, federal and state committees on race relations and job development, or groups involved in cultural empowerment, but those white administrators, politicians, pundits, and personalities who will stand before other whites and present the truth.

The truth is in the 21st Century, the world will continue to diversify and America is ground zero of this international exchange of people, skills, and possibilities. Yet America's means of orchestrating such productivity and potential success is still based on the stereotypes whites have of Black, Latino, Asian, and Indigenous people who have been Americans for centuries. So, there is a need for a shift in how corporations move their organizational cultures. The move should be away from a focus on money alone regardless of who gets hurt, and instead, reimagine a company built on ethics and an understanding of the interconnectivity of various autonomous communities, so they can better meet the needs of people with different views and values. When separate perspectives are held by organizations as possessing equal worth, organizing them into a composite plan, and implementing such a plan will take place comprehensively and cohesively. The key to change lies in remaining consistent, never complacent.

Black executives must fight to maintain pipelines for the development of more diverse inclusion in corporate America. Black executives must learn when to let go of distractions, dead ends, or frivolous debates that could lead to burnout. Instead, Black executives must know when to fall back, regroup, refocus, and either return to the immediate battle at hand or take on a new one. Strategically, Black executives must select different points of focus, plan for potential obstacles in the future, continuously acquire resources, and maintain stability so they will not burnout, they will not be broken,

247

and they will not be denied that championship belt—a position as a senior executive or C-Suite leader. Black executives, don't give in, don't give out, don't give up! Don't throw in the towel. Just return to the ring ready to fight victoriously.

WISDOM TO APPLY IN
THE CORPORATE RING:

• In corporate America, many Black executives don't have cornermen looking out for their best interests. When they throw in the towel, they throw it in alone, and often too late to prevent long-term damage to their careers.

• The attrition rate of Black executives from corporate America is greater than the number of African Americans who are accepted into the senior executive pipeline.

• Like a boxer, the Black executive is often caught between utter defeat, severe injury, or embarrassment to the point where it appears that he or she can't continue. He or she may look to the corner for cues. But even when a fighter feels empowered and believes he or she can overcome the attacks, regain footing, and keep fighting, it often seems wiser to give up rather than suffering serious injury, making it impossible to compete in future contests.

• Many Black executives feel less attached, less bound by the mission and values of their corporations than whites or Hispanics, due to a perceived and actual lack of inclusiveness. Black management, supervisors, and executives report that there is a seedy side of companies in which Black employees are still made to feel like they are "the help" versus being leaders of operations and drivers of progress within their companies.

• Organizations that do more than talk about the challenges Black people face, and instead, take part in providing solutions that address nutrition, training and education, and financial stability can pipeline economically challenged Black children from students to professionals to corporate executives. Such programs should begin as early as middle school and continue through college matriculation, graduation, recruitment, and beyond the point of hire.

• Through Black authenticity in executive leadership, corporate America can approach market segments with authenticity regarding marketing, outreach, utilizing feedback, design, and progress. It's the same with leaders who are white. They may not represent all white perspectives alone, yet they provide applicable insights regarding related demographics within their overall target market population.

BOXING STRATEGY

SMOTHER YOUR OPPONENT'S WORK

Smothering your opponent keeps him from punching and tamps down their aggression. This is a good tactic if your opponent is faster or larger than you, and it allows you to punch without the threat of return punches.

ROUND 10

The Final
BELL

Endurance is the key factor that separates those who spar, those who fight, and those who win. Endurance is often the last thing mentioned among fighters but it is in no way the least important. True, strength, balance, and speed, are the trifecta of skills needed simply to operate around the ring. Taking control also demands the patience to wear down an opponent until a fighter can land the fatal blow or simply outscore the opposition. But even boxers have their limits. The 1982 fight between American fighter, Ray "Boom Boom" Mancini and Duk Koo Kim of North Korea, was the first time that officials recognized that 15 rounds—the official number of rounds prior to this fight—could lead to irreversible brain damage and even death for fighters. Kim was stopped in the 14th round after a grueling fight, and ultimately died of brain damage. By 1988, all major world title fights were reduced to 12 rounds.

Boxing is a sport that sprung from the backrooms of taverns where men of wealth bet on their favorites without regulation. This led to vast corruption allowing wealthy men to promote their favorite fighters and strip worthy opponents of victory based on financial double-dealing and not true ability. By the 1940s and 1950s, the American mob was running the sport of boxing, and federal regulators finally stepped in to protect the sport and fighters from fraud and deceit. Instituting a 12th round for the safety of fighters was one such regulation.

In the field of corporate America, the same gestalt of trial, tragedy, and triumph take place every day, but Black executives cannot rely on regulations and judges to protect their interests. Like the sport of boxing, corporate America is rigged, and those who fall victim to its corruption have a difficult time proving that they were victims of double-dealing because it happens behind closed doors. Black employees at all levels can find their stress levels rise to those of an athlete in a fight or race. In many cases, the ongoing battle wears these employees down and those intent on lasting till the 12th round are often left with permanent damage. Some even die from the strain, whether due to related health issues or by their own hands.

For these reasons, Black executives who want to outlast their opponents must train vigorously to build stamina and endurance. Athletes who are household names such as LeBron James, Serena Williams, or Floyd Mayweather, have all underscored the need to take the nervousness, the jarring emotions, the fear of failure, and funnel them into a form of energy and strength that increases drive, sustains a longing for victory, and, above all, forces the athlete to focus, filter out distractions, and defeat the opponent or the opposing team. In the end, endurance pays off. For instance, maintaining endurance throughout each boxing bout is not merely about outboxing the opponent, but outlasting time, fatigue, thirst, hunger, and blows that seem to come from all directions. This mirrors the psycho-emotional experience of many Black executives, both male and female. Even the most talented executives will have their strength tested within the uber-competitive worlds of American and global business, because nearly everyone is vying for a position on the C-suite team.

The problem is that everyone doesn't start off on equal footing when the fight begins. White traditionalists continue to manipulate the system just enough to keep the mass of Black professionals seeking executive and administrative positions at bay. This constant struggle leads to battles in which the Black executive must always look for opportunities as an individual, within a group, or from an organization that can assist with legal, financial, educational (including training and mentorship), and psychological resources. These resources enable Black executives to regroup, generate and implement strategies, assess results, and forecast the next steps in pursuit of a position, project, or endeavor that showcases their talent and prowess. Further, it supports their candidacy for senior executive positions that even opposing administrative executives cannot deny.

Black professionals are often willing to be the brave ones who take on challenges that many established, white corporate employees refuse to do or steer clear of for a number of reasons. Black executives endure such projects with limited time, tools, staff, finances, and information. Many Black executives are sent on "missions" without the slightest chance of success. Anyone observing such behavior might consider the bravery honorable but the logic questionable. So why take on such a project full of challenges?

First, these are projects no one wants, which provides opportunities for Black executives to perform and outshine fearful or uncomfortable non-Black peers who shy from such a wager. A proactive person does not take on a project to fail. African Americans have always been known to be innovative and make lemonade out of limes. Success starts with a strong will to thrive and train with objectives and goals in mind. The training is not solely to endure but to overcome adversity and be victorious in the end.

As the culture shifts, due to changes in population, influences, and calls for greater equality and diversity, the Black executives will prevail. However, they must continue to endure and overcome the historical lack of representation in executive and C-suite positions.

Black executives must be mindful of the root mentalities that feed into the lack of fairness in organizations that would lead to a greater number of successful Black managers as primary leaders and role models in senior executive positions. Fairness is the clearest sign of equality because the opportunity is in reach of all parties who strive for key positions. Currently, anyone can apply for a senior/C-suite position in any major firm, yet whether they are considered still falls not on their accomplishments, but whether they are liked, respected, and perceived as having the ability to bring people together and best represent the corporate image, operations, and stability of a firm.

The faith that many corporations have in Black leaders is lacking due to white executive leaders struggling with everything from racism and sexism among lower strata employees to their own erroneous apprehension toward fully supporting Black candidates in the multitudes. Again, Latino and Asian leaders may be chosen for the optics. Latino leaders are often seen by corporations as beacons of diversity based on the fact that both English and Spanish are spoken in America. However, few Latinos of color are selected for such positions. Asian leaders are met with more receptiveness from Eastern companies because there is a perception that they may be more advantageous to international business opportunities. Yet, again, other than Asian Indians, few people of color that are distinctly 'Black-looking' are perceived by white executives as potential candidates who can bring various factions within a company together. Aesthetically, most Latino and Asian candidates are lighter and thus can appear "whiter" or seemingly Eurocentric. This is quite offensive and whitewashes the history, perspectives, and even appearance of Latino and Asian Americans.

Often, corporations hire a token African or Caribbean leader meant to appease the growing number of Black professionals who want their shot at the top. West, Central, and Southern Africans have greater cultural ties to white Americans because they go through the British educational system where they learn about white culture, history, and tradition in their homes and communities.

Some African Americans feel that while African and Caribbean professionals embrace their own cultures and ethnicities in their daily lives, when it comes to business, they cater and kowtow to whites and Europeans. This act of accommodating racism to get ahead may be seen by African Americans as selling out. Nevertheless, East Africans, North Africans and those of Afro-Asiatic backgrounds are hired alongside many Arab, West Asian and Central Asian professionals for their potential international appeal, which equals profit when dealing with companies in those nations. That leaves many African Americans feeling left out, overlooked, and surpassed, especially when companies will go outside of the U.S. if they can't find a white executive for the job, they feel they can find an "outsider," "foreign-born" person of color that will be agreeable to certain perspectives that again do not benefit African Americans or Latinos of color-- those concepts, campaigns, or practices founded on racist or racialized sexist ideas.

These ideas continue to dictate the mindset of national and global business, even as the changing social and political topography of America is overturning nefarious concepts about race, culture, and gender. This change has been solely shaped by the efforts of Black professional organizations, educational institutions, and business organizations, which give life to the dead words of Affirmative Action and equal employment opportunity laws, written nearly 50 years ago. With that in mind, the endurance that the Black executive shows will pay off like the endurance of a boxer in the 12th round.

In the entertainment industry, the bias of executives is even more apparent. In entertainment, Black culture has always been a source of style, finesse, and what's been marketed as "cool." Folks love us to entertain them, but lead them into years of success and growth? Oh, no! That's when the racist boxing gloves come out. They sometimes employ a subtle and often more shocking act by simply acting like Black executives don't exist, or they are white executives in Blackface. The war continues, and in some battles, Black executives thrive. Going beyond the dated notion that featuring Black actors in Black movies or shows is progress, Netflix has tackled the real issues and offered Black executives the power they seek. Netflix has heavily invested in Black executives and is currently seeing the expansion in the company's profits (Shamira, 2020).

This profit gain is equaled by the value of its offerings being enriched by various perspectives representing a variety of segments within the target market. With Netflix productions, execs anticipate and address the needs of wide audiences. But, at the end of the day, the color of entertainment is green—money green—and anyone may become a viewer of any show. So, Netflix as a corporation was brave and bright enough to promote the perspectives of Black executives to improve its appeal to various communities of color across the board, leading to financial growth, brand relevance, and dominance over related service providers such as Hulu, Sling, Vudu, Peacock, Apple TV and others.

When there's profit, people apply value. The cultural shift in politics and socialization in America has caused a shift in corporate thinking. Competent companies now understand that they can't keep selling to Black people and not show Black consumers how their interests are potentially reflected in the overall operation, direction, and future of the company (Shamira, 2020).

Netflix is a leading entertainment powerhouse that has come to celebrate African American ingenuity, administration, and vision for the future of the company by addressing the needs of many fans who honor the representation of Black perspectives and values. The unfortunate and seemingly endless string of police shootings, result-ing protests, and conflicts that erupt between protesters, anti-protest-ers, and police/military has made American society take a hard look at itself, and many white Americans do not like what they see and look to people of color, namely African Americans, for some idea of what to do, how to respond, what can be done to move forward.

The pandemic, the racial tension, and the economy have all affected each other as a seemingly deplorable trifecta that has led American businesses to consider getting more Black faces into C-suite positions versus repeating age-old practices with simple-minded views of race, sex, and leadership. Unfortunately, not enough corporations have made the jump. Most have just given lip service and grabbed a few Black actors for "photo ops." Nevertheless, Net-flix serves as an example in their establishment of Netflix's Strong Black Lead marketing team. Netflix has tapped into the reciprocity shared between entertainment and the real world (Shamira, 2020).

Art imitates life, but life often imitates and celebrates art, as well. This celebration of art leads to steady sources of profit from fans. Capitalistic logic would dictate the need for greater inclusion to grow the profit margin of any given business. No matter if a company's white executives are staunch supporters of social change or not, the business of social advocacy leads to executive decisions that impact the direction and future of a firm, franchise, or institution. The narratives told by a culture about itself are authentic. Authenticity leads to greater support by fans, regardless of their cultural background.

The more authentic a narrative, the more believable it is, and the greater impact it has on fans and supporters of that culture, because it gives those external to a culture a more truthful portrayal. Behind truthful portrayals lies individuals who look to progress the development, history, and legacy of people whose voices have been denied or so doctored, their messages, beliefs, experiences, concerns, and motivations become caricatures... which the entertainment world has promoted for years. Nevertheless, Netflix's example is a sign of better things yet to come- a reward following the fight that Black executives continue to endure. The fact is that strong Black leadership best prioritizes the range of Black perspectives and needs (Shamira, 2020).

The impact of the Black dollar was measured in an economic study of sorts when financial watchdog project, My Black Receipt, urged African American consumers to spend $5 million at Black-owned businesses from June 19 (Juneteenth) to July 4, 2020 (My Black Receipt, 2020). Later, the goal of My Black Receipt was increased to collect $10 million in receipts. The purpose of the My Black Receipt project was to reveal the economic impact of the Black dollar on the American economy in real time. In December 2020, the receipts were $7.7 million (My Black Receipt, 2020). Again, when considering African Americans are reported as only 13.4% of the population, their investments/purchases still add up to an impressive $1.3 trillion dollars of the entire U.S. GDP each year and rising (Brown, 2020).

What took place 35 plus years ago continues today. When Black executives grow weary of the games, many start their own businesses or take executive and senior management positions in Black-owned businesses. These Black-owned businesses compete with predominantly white-led corporations, giving them a healthy run for their money and showing them the Black leadership they overlooked and leads to millions that big corporations miss, solely due to the perpetuation of monolithic, mediocre, exclusively white executive leadership. Even in many Black companies, there are, in fact, a number of white employees and leaders as well as others of color that assist in providing various perspectives in which Black business owners understand and utilize to expand their potential to appeal to a wider range of patrons, leading to a larger market share in their particular industry. Yet so many white-led corporations have yet to see the light and fully understand how they are hurting their own business and how incorporating Black C-suite executives would only increase their companies' market values and expand their corporate presence to a greater spectrum of consumers.

Many Black MBAs come out of college and get well-paying jobs only to learn of yet another loophole of marginalization—they can't seem to move up. They become stuck in one position. With no growth, job satisfaction stagnates, and the company takes a loss through wasted talent. The problem is that corporations still do not agree that there are clear advantages to bringing a greater, more diverse group of Black executives into their C-suite positions. Black executives seek out opportunity where they feel they are needed; therefore, many seek opportunities versus creating opportunities in corporations. This approach makes them valuable assets to a company and better prepared to pursue a C-suite position.

In over 35 years, little has changed as far as opportunities for Black executives to move up to senior leadership. According to

Chen and Lucero (2020), it's a matter of personally mediated barriers based on race. Among perioperative healthcare, diversity efforts demand improvement, namely employee and leadership development. However, senior white staff and complacent staff members of color continue to state, "Our specialty doesn't attract people of color; they want to work in primary care and give back to their community." This is an assumption not solely based on statistic but on advisors, counselors, recruiters, employers, trainers, and supervisors steering Black professionals from perioperative healthcare. "We want diversity, but we also want qualified people." Here lies a hollow guarantee of equal evaluation of white and Black candidates, yet from names to alma maters, African Americans are scrutinized against the so-called standard universities, which means white universities, along with those with Anglicized or "white"/non-ethnic names.

Sometimes corporations say, "He or she just wasn't the right fit for our department." When this loaded, packaged response is uttered, there is little investigation into why nor validation that the claim is true. It can come down to mere dislike, distrust, or lack of confidence in a candidate, merely because they are Black. Another phrase uttered by corporate leaders is, "I'm colorblind; I just try to choose the best person for the job." This statement follows when white-executives overlook the experience and formal education of Black candidates. How is such myopic, obtuse, and fallacious thinking justified? It doesn't have to be, which is why it permeates society through social and institutional racism.

It is the "non-racist" racist which aversively accepts the so-called traditionalist system in favor of less movement among Blacks into higher leadership positions, which racists see undermining the progress of American business (Chen & Lucero, 2020). Starting a medical practice demands finances that even the most experienced and brightest Black professionals may not have as individuals. This forces the executives to remain in a position if they want to continue in the field. When the image of leadership is changed, then images of Black leaders become the norm, Blacks will enjoy equal opportunity that does not allow them to be seen as a novelty. This is the objective of the ascending Black executive.

There are no wide range studies that address the number or rate of Black executives lost from white-dominated corporations, because often Black employees go on to become entrepreneurs or later lead Black-owned firms. There are studies that consider actual confirmation of racism and sexism regarding the ascension of populations other than white males. The evidence lies in years of whistleblowing with evidence of recordings showing high-powered senior executives using racist language and suggestive terms that make it clear many corporations are not progressive behind the scenes regardless of claims of diversity, incorporation, and executive leadership development.

The greatest enemy of the Black executive often can be converted into an ally. This enemy-ally is time. Being an available and prized candidate isn't solely based on completing deeds, but making use of publicizing deeds, generating opportunities by supporting certain leaders, using accomplishments as steppingstones, or starting a project based on an accomplishment and using it as a platform that provides the Black executive time to build his or her empire. From that perspective, white executives should be handing Black executives the keys to the C-suite. However, such a progression just hasn't come to pass due to blatant denial of companies reluctant to seriously invest in developing a pipeline for Black employment beyond middle-management. The lack of programs to mentor Black executives as C-suite leaders, which would expand means to incorporate greater Afrocentric perspectives and insights, is evidence that significant support for C-suite development does not exist.

Thirty-five years have gone by and the top floor is still seemingly out of reach. Yet, many times, professionals take another route by developing their own businesses, using their growth and experience to successfully run their own businesses and increase their training and experience. This gives them the needed insight, problem-solving, and delegating skills necessary to meet the needs of customers and generate profit. This is what corporations look for in C-suite executives. But African Americans need to be able to make their own decisions regarding how to pursue progress versus progress being determined through the eyes of white executives.

Since their rise above the proprietorship, partnership, or family business in the late 1890s, corporations gave birth to robber barons: American businessmen who used all forms of underhanded means to rise to the top of the American economy placing their brands in every home across the Nation. These same men also maintained a certain perspective toward leadership and, unfortunately, modeled the views held by the majority of whites at the time, which was in favor of Black labor versus Black leadership. The pervasive belief was that Black's had the brawn to do the heavy lifting, but not the brains for leadership. Why? The fear of being replaced. It has always been about the battle to maintain power.

There are those who, from the founding of their companies, did not support racism, though many may not have been openly supportive of the Negro, later Colored, later Black, later African American cause for equality and empowerment. However, the same companies have supported Black education, voting rights, business development, donated millions to improve the lives of African American communities and enabling a large percent of the success of Black middle-class neighborhoods to date. One business that comes to mind is Microsoft and the philanthropic endeavors of the Bill and Melinda Gates Foundation.

Nevertheless, the need for C-suite positions among Black executives is rooted in the comfort that corporations provide professionals once they are established as leading senior executives. Moreover, the stock options and other opportunities and resources that C-suite positions provide could potentially shift a significant majority of Black median incomes across America. When the earning capacity of a specific demographic increases, those groups will move into higher tax brackets, which gives them a greater voice. That is where the trophy for this 12th round lies—higher earning capabilities and resources that equate to opportunities and balance the economic scales with other racial/ethnic groups. This fight is bigger than a few men or women. This fight is for decades of economic and financial inequality to come to an end. This fight will result in lower representation in government dependency programs. Incidentally, the majority of federal assistance recipients are white women, not single, Black mothers.

Corporate positions come with the same headaches and heartaches an executive might experience while running his or her own business. One set of headaches is simply traded for another. Though in a corporation, there can be more opportunity to develop intellectually, ethically, and ideologically. But the constant shell game of shifting Black executives from one position to another undermines their ability to build merit and tenure in order to further their resume and reinforce their foundation to build toward a C-suite position. A man or women that has run a department for 10 to 20 years is deserving of a senior executive position. However, if a Black man or woman has a 20-year span with a company within a number of departments, their history of leadership over various departments appears inconsistent and scattered. Therefore, many Black executives find that even when they are not stuck in a position, they are still stuck at a certain level within the corporation due to situational obstacles set in place.

Many people do not see the difference between experience running one or several departments. The difference is that while it is good to have experience completing various projects, having an extensive history of administration over one department versus moving from one department to another appears to many competitors, partners, investors, and supporters as consistent and trustworthy. Many Blacks are misled by the belief that leading many departments versus one is comparable, especially when considering how many mediocre people remain in institutions such as American politics for decades and then appear as leading candidates. But mediocrity is less radical and goes along with business as usual with slow or impeded progress, which recently, many brands have been exposed for promoting.

To balance the scales, Black executives who want to be retained in a department position must make that department dependent upon them to the extent that if they were to be transferred, the department would suffer. The means to making a business dependent is by building a network of various demographics that have sustainability and transferability among a spectrum of consumers, partners, investors, vendors, and communities. It's best not to fully disclose detailed plans and approaches that are implemented during operations. If a Black executive is asked to disclose needed information during the start of presentation or defense of a proposal, the answer should be that the information will be limited to what's needed to ground the proposal.

Improvisational leadership is another skill that is rarely taught, but it can be learned through experience. The innate strategic abilities of Black executives are a cultural inheritance, due to racism and years of working with a lack of supplies, support, or platforms. African Americans have always had to innovate with less, and Black innovation has been moving America for centuries; as far back as slavery when Nearis Green, an enslaved man, taught Jack Daniel's how to make whiskey to 2012, when 14-year-old Tony Hansberry II invented a surgical technique that lowers operation time, to the Black inventors of tomorrow (Risen, 2016; Raton, 2012).

One facet of American society that has maintained a potential bridge for more African American professionals to cross into the C-suite lies in the political leanings of the cities where their companies are located. Cities like Atlanta, Chicago, and San Francisco have significantly larger African American populations, and they have experienced a recent wave of more influential Black political leadership, based on the mayorships of Keisha Lance Bottoms of Atlanta in 2018, Lori Lightfoot of Chicago in 2019, and London Breed of San Francisco in 2018. Influential Black leadership leads to ordinances that specify local businesses hire within the surrounding metropolitan area via institutions of higher education. Much like the notorious school-to-jail pipeline that many low-income Black communities experience, Black communities of various socioeconomic status can and have improved corporate hiring. Corporate investment combined with support from local and state governments enables corporations to pull a local employee base from surrounding colleges and universities. The universities and colleges then recruit initially through grade school programs in inner-city and rural communities. Such programs once existed in Cincinnati Public Schools, which would pipeline students to the University of Cincinnati, which in turn led to working for global manufacturer Proctor & Gamble. Even though the local government has historically been conservative since the 1990s, Cincinnati has attempted to generate pathways for African Americans from various socioeconomic backgrounds to employment with P&G manufacturing and management. Yet P&G's executive and C-suite positions remain mostly white and mostly male. Nevertheless, the success of programs that pipeline African Americans to better corporate jobs is evident, especially in cities where Black leadership is the face and direction of social and political change.

The fact is that economic imbalance causes greater strain on our government. When the government backs more contracts to assist historically disenfranchised communities in accessing funds for their businesses or provide funds to support certain levels of diversity within corporations, the result is greater inclusion and greater success. Through this process, the economic resources of populations increase, which takes the strain off of the government services designed to support them. Therefore, in Black-led cities, a Black executive may have a better chance at a senior executive position of a Fortune 500 company in Atlanta versus Portland. However, this is not always the case, nor is the point to condone that anyone should limit themselves to certain areas to live and thrive. Rather, the point is to recognize current resources and alternative means to address the problem of establishing a stable and clear path to senior level management positions as a Black executive.

2020 is the year that the racial affronts experienced by African Americans, Latino Americans, Native Americans, and Asian Americans came to a head. Moreover, Jewish and Muslim communities were under attack. LGBTQ communities came under attack as well. Members who simply agreed with the Left came under attack. From where? The Right. The Right has traditionally been the conservative end of the spectrum and the most influential in the overall structure and function of business as a capitalistic free market. The Republican party is neither good nor evil just as the Democratic party isn't either. But the ideologies that have been expressed by members of the party have further polluted the system of American business and reveal the animus behind police shootings, racist murders, and other acts of blatant racism as well sexism and other forms of bigotry. Therefore, the response to corporate America is a response to contemporary conservative views that reflect underlying racist, sexist, and classist views that remain within the foundation of American economic power.

In 1968, due to the riots and protests in response to the assassination of Dr. Martin Luther King, Jr., Roy Wilkins of the NAACP addressed the American Association of Advertising Agencies (AAAA) regarding Black employment, leadership, and negative images portrayed in advertisement by the market media. A related study took place when the Urban League of Metro New York assessed the ten largest advertising companies to date and discovered that out of more than 20,000 employees, only 0.125% were African American in creative, administrative, or executive positions. Therefore, the NAACP echoed the Urban League's valid argument years before that there is a pressing need for more Black leadership in the Nation's companies to further discourage and deter institutional racism and establish diversity as a common norm within corporate leadership. The same exact issues are a challenge over 50 years later (Glover, 2020).

Strangely enough, Black Baby Boomers, who made great strides in economic, social, and political equality and established themselves in lead executive programs and positions, noticed fewer Black Generation X professionals following their paths in the 1990s. The population flow has dwindled even lower among Black Millennial professionals. Black Millennials are embracing entrepreneurial endeavors at a higher frequency than their economic predecessors. It is due to a need for Black business generated by demands for culturally aware products and services by consumers of color. The entrepreneurial spirit of the Millennial is similar to the Hard Timers generation of the 1920s. However, other than the entrepreneurial spirit, they share a darker connection based on a rise of social racism which has shed a light on the grimy soil-covered foundation of American business and corporations thereof.

The current state of the American racialized economy and its attitudes toward African Americans has reanimated Black-owned businesses, which exclusively serve the Black community—and they are thriving. The racial backlash in American business and society has also led to Black-owned businesses receiving business opportunities and investments by the government as well as private entities working with diverse-owned businesses, thus increasing earning capacities for businesses across the country. Again, many will endure the headaches of business ownership for its rewards versus the false sense of comfort in a corporation that tosses Black executives around until they retire, quit, or are fired.

Black advertising agencies made positive steps, but they fell out of favor. When they did, the advertising professionals who worked for them attempted to return to so-called mainstream agencies but were deemed non-eligible for rehire. Today, the cycle of Black executives leaving mainstream corporate America for Black-owned business continues, which benefits the earning capacity of the Black community as a whole but removes the source for needed Black leadership that will enable American business and thus the economy to grow and further diversify (Glover, 2020).

Another reason Black professionals are turning to Black-owned businesses lies in the concept that their need in corporate America is solely for race relations, essentially keeping Black employees "docile" and working. This perspective is eerily similar to Black overseers of the past. Once Black executives are pigeon-holed as race-relations liaisons, the trap opens, and the cycle continues. In reality, it was racism itself that created the need for race relations, and yet white leadership continues to use Blacks as spokespeople who applaud the company's agenda while assuring other Black professionals that all is well. Fear keeps some Black executives in these overseer or liaison-type of positions, and they are pushed to accept these figurehead positions, preventing them from finding ways to align race relations with operations or administrative platforms. While it may be possible to work this system from the inside, it takes drive, networking, a list of achievements, and above all—time.

Many of the owners and executives of Black advertising agencies never regained much of their business during the 1990s and early 2000s, leading to all forms of tragedy and even the loss of life. However, among Millennials, it appears the entrepreneurial life has become more secure. More access to insurance and the use

277

of loans make it possible for Black Millennial executives who leave their mainstream companies. They already know they have a greater chance to fail than succeed if they focus on going back to work for past companies. Therefore, the motivation to succeed is based in implementing constant, dynamic strategy to acquire finances while securing spending, resources, and their network of patrons, partners, and providers.

There are two forces that face the Black-owned advertiser and those are the conscious corporation with an incorporated diverse leadership network and the average, majority of white-led corporations who have a Total Marketing approach. white-led companies with the Total Marketing approach feel they don't need Black companies or influential African American leadership. Instead of blatant racist refusals, many companies use marketing software and other tools provided by consultant firms to depict and promote their version of Black consumers and communities. However, this marketing push by many corporations is considered insincere and corny by various African American market segments. As Tom Burrell of the internationally known Burrell Communications Group L.L.C. appropriately stated, "Black people are not Black white people" (Glover, 2020).

Recent historical, social, and political strife has shown that endurance has kept the Black executive with his or her feet underneath them, always moving, never standing flat-footed, always anticipating when the next punch or jab will be thrown. They let opponents wear themselves out while preparing a way for the Black executive to land the Coup de Grâce, or death blow, and win. Behold, the age of Corporate Social Justice has arrived.

Companies with Corporate Social Responsibility programs have proven to be more profitable than those who do not see the value in such investments and practices. Since the early 1970s, companies that have utilized such programs have become closely involved in diversity and inclusion work in order to improve their brands and better serve customers. These companies understand skills go beyond mere culture. Skills are not predictable, only applicable. Therefore, in all areas of the nation, companies awakening to the fact that the racism that killed George Floyd springs from the same roots of institutional racism which kills other Black people slowly. Institutional racism impacts African Americans in the most lethal way through missed opportunities and denied rights that affectively rob them of financial, economic, educational, and residential opportunities.

Conscious companies have decided to raise the bar on involvement and development of diverse leadership and specifically Black leadership and representation. These companies are preoccupied with incorporation of more people of color, namely Black people in leadership positions. Within these businesses, Black executives who align their race relations with corporate image and developing the organizational culture are exceling and expanding as their brands increase in popularity and market relevance (Zheng, 2020).

In the age of Corporate Social Justice, companies are reframing their Corporate Social Response in ways that ensure their efforts, investments, and time can be observed and monitored as well as measured. The measurement is based on how companies assist disenfranchised groups, thereby enabling members of the assisted population to report on companies from their own 'assisted' perspectives and assessments.

Companies are realizing that they can perform as social advocates and still meet capital goals in a moral fashion. When companies actually assist populations that they claim to help, their image is vastly improved. These companies understand that what they claim to support must be an authentic representation of what they actually support. Companies that practice Corporate Social Justice understand that Corporate Social Responsibility is integrated into the organizational culture's ethical code. If there is a lack of authenticity, then there is a disconnect between the company and the demographic the company is attempting to secure within its customer base. For instance, Amazon stated its solidarity with Black people and Black Lives Matter, yet it was discovered that Amazon sold facial recognition technology to law enforcement for use in predominantly Black neighborhoods (Zheng, 2020).

Consumers support companies based on brand loyalty versus the transaction of cash for goods or services. Corporate Social Justice dictates that when addressing racism toward African Americans, the response to such attacks should involve Black team members from entry level to executive level, not simply race relations spokespeople. The racial subjugation of Black people through a militarized police force and a judicial system that fails to convict and jail enough police officers for the murder of Black men and women is a key subject of advocacy that a conscious company should take on assertively with a leading team of Black company representatives. Here is where a Black executive can emerge as a leader who can oversee and assess the progress of such programs to further promote that Corporate Social Justice equals incorporation of both internal and external Black stakeholders, from Black employees to the entire community, and their various needs, perspectives, and concerns (Zheng, 2020).

With Black executives at the helm, a company's strategic platforms and resources are more likely to align with its ethical and moral code, which exceeds business alone. The ethical and moral code address the organizational culture of a corporation. Incorporation of African American perspectives, values, and causes shows solidarity and reflects an ethical and moral code that aligns with a corporate image of embracing and supporting diversity beyond the mere customer base.

It takes bravery for corporations to hire Black executives to lead or to donate to causes like Black Lives Matter, because it may offend certain segments of the market, leading to profit loss for the company. However, true loss comes from not standing up. There is more to gain when one group takes heed of how another is treated. The Black community was brought to Americas as a labor force, yet African Americans continue to be treated as if they are invaders. Companies that take a stance recognize that disenfranchisement of African Americans has placed the Black community in historically challenging life situations and environments; thus, it is the duty of American businesses to provide means for their customers to live better and their communities to thrive, which brings companies greater profit and is overall the morality of pluralism. Plurality is the basis and strength of American society (Zheng, 2020).

Conscious companies understand that corporate social justice is an ethical, social, and political partnership with a given community—in this case, the Black community—facing persecution or an adverse issue that demands response. If a company commits to a moral cause but does not address these issues quickly and correctly, further damage can result and target populations are left feeling even more victimized and exploited. Trust must be maintained, starting with the leadership... and when leadership looks more and more like the consumers and communities victimized and marginalized most in America, companies grow, and companies show they are truly for all American people (Zheng, 2020).

In short, Diversity and Inclusion departments need to protect Black employees with regulations like the 12th round. No one fighting for the interest of the company should be expected to sustain ongoing abuse that results in life-changing injuries or career-ending blows.

WISDOM TO APPLY IN
THE CORPORATE RING:

- Like the sport of boxing, corporate America is rigged, and those who fall victim to its corruption have a difficult time proving that they were victims of double-dealing because it happens behind closed doors.

- Black employees can find their stress levels rise to those of an athlete in a fight or race. In many cases, the ongoing battle wears these employees down and those intent on lasting to the 12th round are often left with permanent damage. Some even die from the strain, whether due to related health issues or by their own hands.

- executives who want to outlast their opponents must train vigorously to build stamina and endurance.

- Companies with Corporate Social Responsibility programs have proven to be more profitable than those who do not see the value in such investments and practices.

- Diversity and Inclusion departments need to protect Black employees with regulations like the 12th round. No one fighting for the interest of the company should be expected to sustain ongoing abuse that results in life-changing injuries or career-ending blows.

"

*Black executives
must learn when to let go
of distractions, dead ends,
or frivolous debates that
could lead to burnout.
Instead, Black executives
must know when
to fall back,
regroup, refocus,
and return to the
immediate battle
at hand or take on
a new one.*

"

BOXING STRATEGY

HIT AND RUN

You can either tie up one of your opponent's arms and hit him using your free hand or, when your opponent ties up one of your arms, you hit with your free hand. If your opponent ties you up around your waist, take it as an opportunity to punch with both arms. However you do it, the goal is to hit hard while your opponent is unable to return the punch

Winner
TAKE ALL

"Winner take all" is the point at which a fighter knows he or she is going to win. There is no doubt in his or her mind that he or she will lose. The point is to fight for the title, the purse, and purpose. The purpose above all is the leading reason to fight. The purpose is to be a champion representing the greatness of the art-form, overcoming all inner and outer battles, so that in one moment a man or woman becomes more than human, the boxer becomes the embodiment of drive, strength, style. The master or madam of fighting becomes an icon of power. The will of the spirit to attain and wield this power is based on passion. It is passion that makes men like Ali, Tyson, Holyfield, Leonard, Foreman, Louis, and Ray Robinson legends. The Black executive is the boxer who must have the strength and belief to constantly pursue wisdom in order to thrive. To thrive, the Black executive must improve his or her situation through self-actualization. Through self-actualization, the Black executive can overcome the systemic barriers in place rooted in age old racism and racialized sexism. Whether the battle is short-term or long-term, Black executives must be prepared to battle through heated boardroom arguments to more covert battles that take place through emails. Regardless of the challenge, the Black executive must constantly build networks of allies and resources to battle opponents working against them.

The winner-take-all Black executive understands that he or she must have the mindset of being a "brand of one" then seek out other Black executives as well as allies of all colors who can construct steadfast and loyal networks. However, the boxer, not the trainer, training team, or management is in the ring. Only the boxer stands alone in the ring, but the boxer represents the training, the management, the fans, the brand. The brand we become as individuals represents and sum of our choices, our allies, our enemies, our values for which we stand. The winner-take-all boxer must know this and keep the mind sharp to keep it pure in thought and not be tempted to take a selfish or quick opportunity. Taking the selfish or quick opportunity is based in making a silent agreement. This agreement can lead one down dark path into the heart of challenges. These challenges are based on trading integrity simply for income or influence.

The Black executive seeking to win it all understands he or she cannot get ahead working for someone else's dream. One must come from behind the shadows of supporting that gives them no fortune nor return. The only time working for someone else's dream is good is for the purpose of faith or charity; corporate America serves neither. Therefore, the object in corporate America should be winner-take-all, not in a greedy way, but a deserving way. Only by reaching and maintaining a position at the top will a Black executive excel long enough to pave the way for the growing Black executive generations that follow. Black people at any level need to understand that working for others' dreams makes them "employ-ee-preneurs." You never get ahead as solely an employee or exten-sion of someone else's dream or plan. This is why any and all Black professionals must push forward with the mindset of an executive, a leader, leading themselves to greater accomplishment, opportunity, and responsibility. Pursuing a dream that is not your own is detrimental. Always work for yourself, your benefit, your growth this is the measure of one's independence no matter if they are an entrepreneur or striving corporate tycoon.

One Black executive who awakened to her own greatness to move from an entrepreneur to a corporate tycoon was Barbara Gardner Proctor. Proctor trailblazed not only for Black men and women. Starting in 1969, Proctor was a barrier-breaking ad agency executive that took America by the collar, stunning both supporters and opponents alike. Proctor is seen as a pioneer in ad agency equality. She got tired of sitting at the "proverbial" lunch counter ready to be served. Being served would mean Proctor would've been allowed to work her craft, grow as a businesswoman, and expand. But racists and sexists have always been predictable when it came to opposing Black people especially Black women. Proctor packed her bags and took her skill and grace to a new platform in which she would be the corporate leader versus a diva of entrepreneurship alone (Genzlinger, 2019).

In 1969, Proctor refused to walk up and down Chicago streets for an advertising agency that sought to parody the social justice marches of Civil Rights, Black empowerment, and the Black Revolution in a racially-charged campaign for Black haircare products. Proctor understood had she chosen to take on the campaign, she would've put herself in danger and been ridiculed for years by the Black community as well as others conscious of the racist plot. It would've been like mocking the BLM, NFAC, or any Black movements of today. Some range from non-violence to exercising the Second Amendment right. No one with any sense of any race would openly make fun of Black sociopolitical movements without expecting a harsh response including boycotts. Based on Proctor's refusal, she was fired (Genzlinger, 2019).

Profoundly, Proctor realized that if she did not control her destiny--her very future, the course of her life would change every five years... The revolving door of entry-level to management-based jobs would've been Proctor's norm. Proctor didn't consciously think that she would be the first Black woman in America to establish her own ad agency; yet she was, starting the ad agency under the name Proctor & Gardner. Proctor was actually Barbara Gardner's married name. Barbara Proctor had divorced her husband some years before, but instead of returning to her maiden name, she kept Proctor as her last name. Due to the sexism along with the racism, Proctor decided to use her maiden and married name together to present the appearance of a male partner. Years later, Proctor & Gardner became a multi-million-dollar industry (Genzlinger, 2019).

With an $80,000 loan, Proctor was able to land her first major account with Chicago's Jewel Foods. Proctor later landed deals with Kraft Foods and Sears Roebuck & Company. By 1984, she became well-known for her appearance on *60 Minutes* and recognition by President Ronald Reagan. President Reagan was notorious for his racist and sexist slights, but in the case of Proctor, he stated she had risen from meager beginnings, "…[in the] ghetto to build a multimillion-dollar advertising agency in Chicago" (Genzlinger, 2019). True, the description reads with a very condescending tone; however, it is still a recognition by white traditionalists that Black ingenuity was valuable and was not something to ignore. However, many white traditionalists see Black ingenuity as a threat to their power structure or a tool of commercial opportunity.

As both a threat and a tool, Proctor & Gardner was a focus of white competitors who felt they could save money by hiring their own advertising teams focused on non-whites, namely Blacks. Many of these teams were devoid of Black people which is terribly counterintuitive. Most of these teams in the 1980s up until the early 2000s were merely a hodgepodge of whites who felt they could generate cheap, marketable images of Black people to market to Black people; however, these images were still familiar enough to white consumers based on the images' skewed presentation African Americans. These skewed images had roots in 1950s advertising which was based on even more distorted and racist imagery long before Black people were considered "Americans". Proctor continued building and expanding relentlessly. Proctor & Gardner ended in the late 1990s (Genzlinger, 2019).

Beyond being a trailblazer, Proctor is noted as a staunch leader in conscientious advertisement. Upon her example, many Black advertisers and even corporations that consider themselves socially conscious avoid advertising any products or services that are detrimental toward women and African Americans such as cigarettes, alcohol, and other products aligned with poor physical, mental, or spiritual health, (Genzlinger, 2019).

With a winner-take-all mentality, Black executives, past and present have always had a sense of empowerment even when they were told by white traditionalists that they had no power. The difference between trailblazers and heroes of Black leadership and those professionals who believed the "bs"—"biased **scrutiny**," is that the trailblazers and heroes always know the truth. The truth was and remains that the white traditionalists are full of it and their entire power structure has been based on years of lies filled with racist and sexist notions for every individual other than a White, Anglo-Saxon, male Protestants.

The sense of self-righteousness that white traditionalists continue to promote is a coping technique to employ while trying to make racist and sexist notions acceptable norms. White traditionalism is similar to Kipling's notion of the "white man's burden," the burden of Europeans and Caucasians to assist the world's people of color by imposing "white civilization" as the will of God, a reference to the twisted notion that white people are God's chosen people. We are all God's chosen people, but what some people have done with the wisdom and freewill God has bestowed on nations around the world is by far sinful and sacrilegious.

The white traditionalist sense of self-righteousness works off of exploiting the challenges people of color faced centuries ago and using divide and conquer to take control over all of the warring nations of color. This erroneous belief derives from the Eurocentric view of people of color as inferior. White traditionalists and some of the best leaders of worldwide companies feel justified in limiting the power and influence of others because they feel innately superior. However, the basis upon which the so-called best leaders were chosen was defined by white men only, making the notion fallacious. The fallacy is evident since the workforce and consumers who center around brands are not solely white men or white people.

Black executives with this knowledge and insight make moves striving for leadership regardless of the sacrifice. These are the Black executives who live the "winner-take-all" life. Nevertheless, the number of Black executives specifically in senior and C-suite positions remains low, and instead of being a few prize-winning boxers, the metaphor for the winner-take-all Black executives should be a highly trained and capable army of soldiers. As soldiers, these Black executives can and will tear down the barricades of racism and racialized sexism. Once the barricades are torn down, witnessing Black executives in action will become more of a norm and less of a novelty.

Black leadership in corporate America is a matter of empowerment that goes beyond merely wanting to increase financial and capital gain. Whether it's stock options, parking spaces, or some other perks that come with a job, the Black executive with the winner-take-all mentality is fine with such things, but he or she takes action to build not to simply acquire power or resources. One major result of the Black executive building is the establishment of foundations for the next generation of professionals. The foundation of stronger, more progressive networks counter systemic racism and sexism, allowing for more Black executives and other executives of color to manifest greater accomplishments in a dynamic commercial and economic landscape. The Black executive who is a winner-take-all warrior fights for the purpose of being known as the best and standing above all the competition for more than the championship itself. Such boxers win as champions to overcome negative notions of inferiority. The winner-take-all boxer fights with purpose, seeking to destroy all doubt of his or her capability to be the best.

Nevertheless, there is always consideration of the dirty hand in boxing. The dirty hand is the hand that's in place to make trouble for the Black executive as the boxer. The dirty hand represents unfair business moves made on behalf of the opponent. Other than the World Professional Boxing Federation and the United States Boxing Council, there is little regulation in boxing. The only regulation is the essentials such as licensing, rules of engagement, what is considered a legal or illegal blow, observing doping (anti-drug) laws, and observing the need for boxers to be disease-free, specifically blood-borne viruses, as well as Coronavirus. As far as regulation regarding behavior, sincerity, and rules of engagement, there's a disconnect. The indicator that this is true lies in the dirty hands we are familiar with such as the unscrupulous promotors, referees, and judges who meet in clandestine restaurants or hotel lobbies for exclusive discussion of how fights should play out. The dirty hands discuss how to sell certain fighters as champions while holding others back through deception forcing them to lose. Boxing is not like the world of wrestling.

The WWE and AEW represent professional wrestling, but professional wrestling relies more on the gimmick, the theater, the presentation of a performance that entertains versus the perceived seriousness and history of boxing. However, promoters such as Don King or Bob Arum, embody the dirty hand turning away from integrity, instead, making sure to put on a show but not a fair fight. Both King and Arum were known for working for and against their boxers depending on how much they valued the boxer for regarding cash. Both King and Arum undermined the futures of countless boxers who never would make it to high-publicity, high-end prize fights. The dirty hand is seen in all areas of business. Whether it's corporate America, the music business, or even government contracting, there is always the potential for the dirty hand in favor of unfair advantages to undermine otherwise worthy, well-rounded professionals. This scenario continually affects Black professionals adversely when they ascend to management and later seek executive and senior executive positions.

The winner-take-all boxers are more focused on what prize fights get out of them than what they get out of the fights. What the fights bring out are the means for winner-take-all boxers to know themselves, know their strengths, their areas of needed improvement, and the areas in which the boxers can help others. The primary area of aid is for the winner-take-all boxer to inspire others to fight and grow. The winner-take-all boxer understands with every obstacle, with every opponent conquered, the boxer becomes a champion based on what he or she overcomes. Adversity introduces a person to him or herself. When boxers, set on the championship, seek to build fights, often their trainers and promoters will set them up with journeymen fighters. Though considered mediocre or middle-of-the-road entertainers, the journeyman provides a level of fighting above sparring partners. Often the journeyman or journeywoman is still a fighter by profession and can still be a challenge for a developing boxer. However, it is up to the boxer to keep in mind that the goal is to grow as a fighter by building resilience for the next battle.

In the *Matrix Reloaded* (2003), the character Seraph fights Neo and is nearly defeated before Seraph submits, later stating, "You do not truly know someone until you fight them" (Wachowski & Wachowski, 2003). However, whether in life or boxing, you do not truly know yourself until you fight for something beyond yourself. One man who fought for more than money, a position, or perks, and instead chose to fight for the purpose of proving white traditionalists in corporate America wrong was Derek Walker.

Derek Walker was one Black executive who rose up from the ranks, meeting challenges head on and always approaching the corporate game as a champion. He stood among competitors that he felt needed to prove their worthiness to work alongside him. Walker took on the more prolific path of pushing himself as a Black executive. He refused to prove his worth by seeking approval from the same white traditionalists who fought him tooth and nail simply to do his job as a lead advertiser. Currently, Walker uses his power as an influencer to improve the success of Black professionals that seek his tutelage. For over 30 years, Walker has remained a force of influence and impact on the overall vision and view of American advertising (Shelton, 2021b).

Walker overcame his first major challenge through determination and charisma. Walker sought to enter a business program through advancement placement. However, the business school stated that all students had to go through the entire program, starting in the freshmen year. Walker already had the classes and credentials. He convinced the administrators of the Georgia-based program that he was far more qualified than a student entering as a freshman. He deserved to enter the program as a junior. He was able to persuade the administration. Walker knew what he was doing and established his worth as an asset to the school. As a student, he would reflect the effectiveness of the school's program. The school understood this and obliged Walker's desire. He began the program as a junior with all his previous credits and courses recognized.

Walker's fellow students were younger, affluent, and white. They had half of his experience. Yet, they saw Walker as a target of their foolishness. One white student stated that Walker, who hadn't been through the freshmen and sophomore courses, had been dropped in with the sharks. Walker stated clearly, "I am white-trained, but Black-raised and there's only one creature that is Black and white that kills sharks." The audacious arrogance of the young-er, white student left his face as Walker sat down confidently. In terms of marine animals that eat and destroy sharks, the orca comes to mind. Orcas as a pack or individuals use speed, agility, and power to hit and stun sharks, leaving them vulnerable to be bitten, disabled, and turned into orca food. Walker continued his campaign to shut down insults and assumptions about him, stating to the young, white student, "They didn't drop me in here with you. They dropped you in here with me." Psychologically, the white ridiculers were conquered as they began to focus on their own inadequacies against a more senior student. Soon, they stopped attempting to make Walker feel out of place. Walker took the power away from them because he used his power to succeed and surpass all competition.

Walker felt that access to the competition made him shine brighter versus shy away from a challenge. Walker felt that the competition--the white traditionalists--had and continued to build fences to keep them safe from being outperformed by Black professionals. It was never a matter of White people being better or stronger; they had just convinced everyone else to believe the lie versus compete for the champion title. Black people always had the grind and grit in them to build, conquer, and lead. Walker refused to be a token; he raised the bar by becoming the standard. The competition needed to keep up with him. Considering athletes, Walker did for advertising what Ali did for boxing, what did Jackie Robinson did for baseball, what did Jordan did for basketball...or what Tiger Woods did for golf. Woods didn't integrate golf. He improved it despite the racism against him. He raised the bar and made the racists shut up, sit down, and take notes.

Walker understood that when the weight is taken off, Black people thrive in epic fashion. Yet, the current reality is that we continue to operate in corporate America as well as most of society within pockets of isolation, and we still manage to achieve greatness. Therefore, we must continue to change the game until the haters, the opponents, and the white traditionalists can't change the rules anymore. Once the rules can't be changed, no one will compete with unfair advantages. At that point, the white traditionalists will be so outmaneuvered, they will have to play on level playing field with everyone else.

If corporate America was the NBA, Black professionals as basketball players would need to face the rim versus posting up with their backs to it. We are told to anticipate one form of offense, so we prepare with a certain defense. Yet, within that defensive stance, we miss opportunity to turn over the ball and score with the opportunity to succeed. We only stand with our backs to the rim to defend. Black people like the basketball player or boxer need to reflect on past wins and learn from them. At the same time, we need to contemplate loss and seek lessons of depth thereof. Too many times, Black people don't see the value of our achievements because we continue to allow white traditionalists to downgrade and narrow our perspectives, regarding our morals and values upon which we measure success. This recollection of success is a matter of turning a toe-to-toe conflict around in our favor with a winner-take-all mentality.

Walker noted that white people are often not qualified for an immediate position, but they are "grown" into a position; they receive training and support to "grow" into the position. However, Black people are not groomed; most are expected by white traditionalist administrations to be fully prepared with training and experience to be in a position. Blacks are not afforded the benefit of potential or room to grow into positions, we have to be ready-made for high-level management and executive positions. Walker pointed out the need for equal access to jobs based on equal assessment of all people. Race and gender don't matter when everyone is assessed the equally.

Black executives must draw attention to removing so-called microaggressions from the job as well as society because these "aggressions" are not "micro" to the victim of such elusive "hate

303

crimes." For instance, racism and sexism are evident when thousands of current corporations still state what's passionate for white men is considered aggressive in Black men and considered negative and emotional in Black women. White women still face marginalization, but again they share in white privilege by proxy based on their association with white men. White people are trained for C-suite positions without consideration of systemic limitations whereas Black people while training for senior-level positions train with limitations in mind. Regardless of their training and experience, many Black professionals are simply not selected based on deep-seated distrust and insincerity whites feel toward and share with Blacks.

Black people in general have always sought for society to reflect our value of accepting so-called outsiders into our areas, communities, cultures, resources, values, and needs. It is like playing basketball at the park in every Black neighborhood. Blacks, for the most part, allow players passage as long as they come to play—no matter their race or gender. Simply put, if a "dude" or "chick" can ball, they are provided access to do so. However, in the white neighborhoods where Blacks would attempt to play ball, most Blacks were and continue to be stopped, searched and arrested by cops, or attacked or chased by the white thugs set on knocking some Black, Brown, or Yellow heads. The same is true for corporations. A white man has a bad day, he's given a free pass and an explanation by the predominantly white administration. The white man in question is said to simply be dealing with some challenges, and he'll be functional in no time. However, if a Black man has a bad day, he is threatened by transfer, demotion, or worse with little to no benefit of the doubt.

According to Walker, Black executives should work like Black street ball players looking to play on the white neighborhood basketball courts, not because the competitors are any better; rather, it's for the better-quality resources—better opportunities to grow, succeed, and exceed the level they would have reached on Black basketball courts alone. Obviously, this is a metaphor and not always the truth. There are Black neighborhoods that are economically stronger than many white neighborhoods. However, in comparison, Black neighborhoods experience adverse economic impact compared to white neighborhoods across America.

Beyond the metaphor, Black executives must understand we are better candidates for so many positions we are denied because we have completed equal to or surpassed the accomplishments of many white contemporaries—regardless of the handicaps placed upon us by white traditionalist society. We must never work for validation by others; instead, we must build and add value to companies and benefit personally from our hard work. We must build our companies around us and our needs versus building a career around how much our company chooses to need us. When that need is not in our favor, we suffer. We must never make that mistake. We must be boxers who fight for ourselves and represent the greatness of the boxing world. We must not fight for a league until we are worn husks of the prize fighters we used to be only to be tossed aside and replaced.

As a Black executive with a winner-take-all mentality, one must never compromise based on criticism alone. It only leads to a chain of compromises that are centered on discrediting and quieting the Black executive despite the strength of his or her plan. Later, the same compromises are expected by white traditionalists that will always challenge the Black executive. From that point, Black executives establish constant compromise that adversely works against any plan, request, idea, or need they possess. Thus, compromises can only be made when they maintain the satisfaction of all parties involved, noting the needs of all parties are met to the fullest.

Many would state compromise is necessary to business. However, instead of one or both sides losing anything by compromising, the focus should be negotiating where everyone wins. Negotiation is necessary, but only when one is not negotiating from a point of loss, specifically when it comes to self-respect. We must never compromise our self-respect; that is our spirit. Peace cannot be gained at the price of compromise rooted in attack upon us. There are other companies and other jobs. There are courts ready to bring racists and sexists to justice when racists and sexists refuse to stop their path of destruction within companies in which Black professionals have invested talent and time.

We need to look at the conditioning we receive going into corporate America. We as Black executives need to study how corporate America works, then we will recognize the fallacies we have accepted as normal for generations. The biggest compromise is accepting the systems of fallacy that arose from overt racism and became the systemic racial roots of American economic success. Yet as the lies continue to be thwarted, the white traditionalist grip on the American economy is slipping, not only nationwide, but worldwide.

We as Black people need to battle within the parameters of the game but at the same time address the falsehoods within the rules and even the purpose of the game. This game is the system. Systemic racism exposed by Black executives in any conflict with white traditionalists is a matter of addressing the falsehoods within the game and thus why the system. We need to call out anything we find offensive without fear of how we will be perceived or received.

Black people must remain unapologetic when we make a statement referring to any violation we see against our race, cultures, ethnicities, manhood, womanhood, family structures, children, or beliefs in any religion.

When we know it is clearly a "hate on Blacks" moment, we need to nip it in the bud, expeditiously. If not, Black professionals become victims of anxiety. This anxiety is what holds us back from facing who and what marginalizes and disenfranchises us in the system. The fear of reprimand from predominantly white leadership in corporate America is based on the fear of loss but working in fear is not healthy nor sustaining. Working within a hostile environment is a matter of abuse. The Black executive, male or female, is like an abused woman in a relationship. The woman is worried about losing "her" man, but if her "man"—the job—doesn't change, the abuse continues. The woman who is strong leaves and rebuilds her life (a new career) because she loves herself enough to be resilient and continue to grow. This is how the Black executive must act when faced with working in an abusive, hostile work environment.

Dealing with racism and pushing back is always a difficult decision, but it's necessary when it comes down to the wire. Nipping a few comments in the bud, to legal action, to even self-defense can become points of serious consideration. You are important. Respect is a form of protection, and when people violate that barrier of protection, you defend it to the fullest. Games played that are racist should always be addressed, matching aggression with aggression. That is when the line is drawn. No racist or sexist shall prosper when people put self-respect before a job. It's a matter of morality, self-love, and belief in a higher power.

The Black executive must remember never to allow any jokes or anything that implies harm to go unchallenged without a formidable response of defense. Black people must protect themselves at all times, no different than any other group of people. Black executives must understand self-preservation. When the Black executive has to explain why such a response was given to a white traditionalist, the Black executive should never hold back when addressing the violation.

The Black executive needs to understand defense is a matter of being ready to fight at all levels; however, legal is the best, but the battle begins with the mind. It begins with the goal of combat to end the conflict. Ending the conflict, leads to an enemy defeated and a precedent set to be left alone and understood. The understanding is the Black executive will be respected at the cost of losing his or her job. This could include harm to the company or members themselves if they should be disrespectful. No matter the job, if there is a personal sense of threat, a Black executive needs to take action and confront the white traditionalist or sympathizer of color who may present potential harm. It should never get to this level; however, self-preservation is everything. Take any threat as serious, never a joke.

From self-preservation to Sarbanes-Oxley, whistleblowers are protected and grasp the need to protect themselves. It is not best to just blow up after holding back. Establish that you will not tolerate abuse or disrespect, document all incidents, and build a case based on logs (emails, recordings, or data). Establish a paper trail to present to HR so that it doesn't seem emotional or vindictive. That is a common stereotype about Black men and women when faced with conflict: their reactions are not cognitive or logical but rooted in emotion and psychological instability. Logically, anyone knows that isn't correct, but many white people are culturally wired to perceive Black emotional expression as more amplified and often alarming based on the older misbelief that less passionate, more docile Blacks were safe and predictable. This racist perception continues into the present. With the validation of documentation, a Black executive cannot be thwarted. The strategy is to turn racists on themselves by owning their falsehoods and abuses. Even with a settlement to leave or to stay, it is best to always have a lawyer ready. It's best to never discuss top end responses from allies at places of business. Rather, it's best to have them email how they feel.

The limit of abuse is based on how long the victim allows the abuser to continue as this is compromising to what the abuser wants. The abuser wants the victim to compromise the safety, security, and respect. To battle the abuser, it's a matter of thinking outside the box and not fearing the potential loss of a job, rather, Black executives need to think like boxers and consider losing the fight. You can lose the battle but still win the war. You don't truly lose the fight when you learn something from it. When you learn about obstacles and opportunities you can flip to your will, you generate a stronger character and multifaceted strategies. The greatest champions lost prize fights, but they never lost themselves. Instead, they learned from the fight and freed themselves with the knowledge that they would not fall in the future. They learned how to roll with the punches... We may fall but rise again and know we cannot be conquered by our burdens. We don't know how strong we are until strength is our only option. That can be fighting off the enemy, fighting off disease, or fighting off doubt, despair, and depression. We must be the boxer that keeps getting off the floor, learning from falling, but always focused on getting back up. Derrick Walker said plainly, "There are better lessons in losing than there are in winning."

Living to battle another day is based on learning from mistakes, but also, we must learn from our accomplishments and maintain a foundation that enable us to continue to rise up. From that foundation, we know we will survive and later thrive. Never lose the fight against yourself. Never compromise your peace. Let stress go before stress lets you go. This could mean sickness or death. Worry is a down payment on what may or may not happen. Fear is fake evidence appearing real. We can't let fear make us focus on losing. The fearless focus on winning.

We have to evaluate our situations at work based, outside of the company's perspective of our employment. We are more than assets; rather, the company is a resource for us. We add to the resource and receive reward in return. This takes away some anxiety about money and not allowing the idea of money to control us. Money is a resource. Its value is based on awareness. Awareness impacts how we develop networks, learn strategies, improve delivery, and enrich presentation as Black professionals.

At times, the fight is not about blatant disrespect, rather, it may be an opportunity to correct a racial or racialized fallacy through instruction. The instruction's intent is to inform, include, and invite white people to learn. This is what gets white traditionalists thinking and some considering "white transitioning." White transitioning is a transition from a traditionalist mentality to a pluralistic perspective. The white pluralistic perspective is culturally aware, culturally relevant, and culturally inclusive. These are the white allies that embrace differences not solely to learn but to best interact and involve others, specifically Black people. The connection that many allies seek is based on the Black exchange of trust and maintaining that trust. White allies learn how to better their relationship with Black people by interacting with peers on the job if not in their own communities. It is the job of white pluralist executives to assist Black executives in the battle against white traditionalist pushback; otherwise, those so-called pluralist allies are not serving their purpose and are not sincere.

Black executives need to look out for one another. We need to serve each other as counselors and respect each other's insights, which leads to a better defense as a force going into a battle or support in celebration of our individual triumphs. We can battle alone, but we must fight for the entire Black professional community itself. We don't have to respond with a thunderbolt-filled power punch every time we battle, but we must throw a jab, a shot, a crossover, or an uppercut to set the opponent up for the knockout. Each punch causes damage when there's strategy behind them. Fight to end battles, not to prolong them. The quicker the battle is the better, but never rush it. A fighter must be patient and let the battle move with the time needed. Keeping the enemy at bay is never good. Fight to end attacks. When imposed upon, it is best to attack until the enemy stops. When the enemy chooses new tactics, we must adapt to thrive victoriously.

We must always beware of the punch we don't see coming. Again, the unseen punch is like the dirty hand. Therefore, it is best to check and assess the loyalty of our team. As Black executives, we need to be loyal and be open to assessment of our loyalty by our brothers and sisters in the struggle. As a team, Black executives support each other, noting the potential for team members to be attacked by unseen fists and knocked out. We need to continuously train each other and inform each other of new developments and access to resources and strategies. Access to new resources and strategies will ensure our continued success as we battle opponents and their unscrupulous forces. We need to always strive to land the winning punch.

Black executives have to identify their needs in their own

voice. Defining ourselves, our needs, and our purpose assists in establishing connections with non-Black allies versus allowing racists to continue their malevolent narrative of Black professionals in corporate America. Black executives cannot be quiet because white people need to know when their presentation to or interaction with Black people is offensive, plain and simple. People, regardless of race or gender, won't like everything said, but if there is no lie or malice involved, then what a Black executive says--responding to racist or sexist acts--is the truth. If a room of board members, administrators, or executives attempt to sweep such violations aside, it's time to hit them where it really hurts—in their pockets.

We behave based on what we believe. We limit our behavior and beliefs when we continue to think within the parameters of the oppressors. We see the oppressors as gate keepers versus invaders who need to be removed. The invaders capitalize on the ingenuity and labor of those denied equal pay, equal power, and equal priority regarding the function and future of American society. The Black executive must protect the gains of Black people from consumers to C-suite leadership. We must protect what's ours--our treasure. That is what the Black executive needs to reach for and fight for: continuous attainment of high-level Black leadership in senior, C-suite executive positions throughout all of corporate America (Showtime, 2021).

We must also remember to fight toward a goal which we can continuously improve versus fighting with a reference constantly connected to a painful past or list of adverse experiences. We cannot be affective if we constantly fight from a point of pain, weakness, or trauma versus fighting toward a point of peace, prestige, and prosperity for Black people in America and abroad. We must always fight with Black America in mind. The RZA said it best, "When we move together, the world moves" (Showtime, 2021).

WISDOM TO APPLY IN
THE CORPORATE RING:

• The winner-take-all Black executive understands that he or she must have the mindset of being a "brand of one" then seek out other Black executives as well as allies of all colors who can construct steadfast and loyal networks.

• Black leadership in corporate America is a matter of empowerment that goes beyond merely wanting to increase financial and capital gain. Whether it's stock options, parking spaces, or some other perks that come with a job, the Black executive with the winner-take-all mentality is fine with such things, but he or she takes action to build not to simply acquire power or resources.

• As a Black executive with a winner-take-all mentality, one must never compromise based on criticism alone. It only leads to a chain of compromises that are centered on discrediting and quieting the Black executive despite the strength of his or her plan.

• We have to evaluate our situations at work based, outside of the company's perspective of our employment. We are more than assets; rather, the company is a resource for us. We add to the resource and receive reward in return.

BOXING STRATEGY

PUT THE PRESSURE ON

Keep the pressure on your opponent with the goal of tiring them out. You want your opponent to feel like they are losing and that there's no way to make a comeback. When you see your opponent start to fade, take it up a notch and finish the job.

ROUND 12

How to be a
CHAMPION

Boxers fight for a lot of reasons. For some it's money, for others, fame. Some come up scrapping in tough neighborhoods where fighting is mandatory for survival, and boxing offers a more acceptable way to channel their skills. In truth, it doesn't matter why they step into the ring the first time; but what they hope to achieve by being there. Are they fighting just to stay in the ring and see how far they can go, or are they one of the rare few who know, deep down, that they will never be content until they are a champion?

Champions are a rare breed, because for them, good enough is never good enough. It takes endurance and strategy to become a champion, but it also takes unrelenting passion, conviction and determination. Champions fight with their minds as often as they fight with their fists, and when they are outmatched, they dig deeper and find fortitude in their own unwillingness to be second best.

The same is true for Black executives in corporate America. Blacks cannot reach the upper echelons of corporate leadership without the inner resolve to keep fighting until they do. At some point, every Black executive realizes they aren't just fighting for their own careers but for the right of every Black person to rise as far as their talent can take them. Being a Black champion in the corporate world means overcoming impossible odds while also opening new doors for those fighters who will come after them. Tom Burrell is one such man.

Tom Burrell is an icon of Black advertisers and an early champion of diversity in marketing. Being a champion demands endurance and strategy above everything. His start stretches back 60 years ago to 1961. He moved from mailroom to Junior Copywriter, then worked for Leo Burnett, then Foote, Cone, & Belding in London, back to Needham, Harper, & Steers, and then launched his massively successful Burrell Communications in 1971. He is the originator of the modern approach to marketing regarding diversity and the African American consumer with his catch phrase, "Black people are not dark-skinned white people." He overcame obstacles beyond discrimination. He overcame possibility blindness, moving forward, and leading a legacy. That legacy continues in the present day at Burrell Communications. Burrell was a champion because he created a self-sustaining network, a legacy that evolves so it thrives. Burrell's example for Black executives is to be innovative, forward-thinking, and a risk taker who understands his or her niche.

The African American consumer is the focus of diversity and inclusion because it is a market. Yet, at one time it was niche. Not that niches are not important, but until there is some demand for change from consumers within the niche, corporations will simply market to niche consumers as the companies see fit. In other words, Burrell based his success by shifting the African American consumer as a niche demographic to a market where he revealed the need for change when the Black dollar grew in demand. This demand exploded during the 1980s due to a strong economy at the time that sustained a larger Black middle class. Legal action led to more opportunities for better jobs and a shift in views regarding how Black consumers spent their dollars. They wanted quality products provided by brands reflecting Afrocentric values and solidarity to representative marketing. The Black dollar became a market because its value was based on the Black community's need of authenticity. Here is where Burrell thrived and represented how to be a champion.

Tom Burrell expert, Dr. Jason Chambers, stated that the Black executive needs to have the opportunity to lead, but also the opportunity to fail, succeed, move forward, and to grow. The outcome must be positive, but the industry was designed to keep Black people out. All aspects of American culture have been stratified to disenfranchise African Americans and place the greatest burden through the generation and enforcement of laws. American society is not simply based on laws. Its infrastructure is based on money. Therefore, every American who pays any tax should have a substantial amount of input as a stakeholder and shareholder in the federal government. Yet, even though the private sector and, directly and indirectly the federal government love the Black dollar, they do not always show the same love to the Black people spending them.

Times are changing in America politically and socially, though, and social justice has become a substantial tool of change to force companies to progress in their cultural development of inclusion and incorporation. Current priorities for inclusion and incorporation are driving Black executive empowerment, adding Blacks to the workforce, and providing opportunities that reflect racial equity among all employees.

In banking, engineering, and design, Black people have excelled because similar to advertising, they can inform, instruct, and sell to their own. Black people essentially have served as a labor source and now a financial source, which is limited by their means of labor. Yet, collectively, their buying power is worth $1.4 trillion dollars. Without individual means of maintaining substantial incomes and properties, Black people have been limited to only a few opportunities for leadership while white traditionalists have maintained a substantial amount of influence. This influence is manifested in power. Advertising, whether public or private, has always been an exclusive business led by white men for white people catering to mostly white women versus Black men and women. Therefore, in order for advertising to succeed it has to reflect the sociopolitical culture and events of the time in order to succeed. Advertising and society have a reciprocal relationship based in how they influence each other. This would explain why we are feeling this shift in tactics. More civil unrest and political change forces companies to be more accountable and maintain solidarity with their customer base or they'll lose their customer base—lose money. So, like the boxer who needs to match the fighting spirit and win to maintain the support of his or her fans, Black leadership must be Black-led in collaboration with white pluralist executives to enhance, enrich, and expand the earning capacity and development of corporate America.

However, the current state of most corporations regarding the diversity of its senior leadership is lacking. People get discouraged because of all the false walls placed in front of them no matter how far they progress. This is what leads to Black professionals leaving corporate America. The closer you get to the seats of power, the more you realize that the sharing of power is not what it seems. Corporations claim they want to change, but not enough to be significantly inclusive, incorporating Black leadership. The solidarity that corporations claim with Black consumers and professionals is embargoed and imbalanced. The corporations claim they want to change their culture, but their actions don't reflect it.

Your actions must speak louder that what you say and advertising has been designed to focus on the demographic of the consumers which began with racist and sexist notions excluding others who were diverse or seen as external of the "focus culture." In 2021, the fact that Black people can still say, "I'm the first Black..."" re-inforces the fact that racism is real in America and throughout the world. Due to the evident social and political change and demand for corporations to be accountable for their stand for social justice, the pressure for proficient performance is greater than ever. This performance must be translated to more than a few Black spokespeople; the need is for Black influence throughout all processes of corporate America from operations to finance, administration to acquisitions. At the present, what is taking place regarding racial equity, especially in leadership, will be the foundation for the next generation of Black executives, deans, and presidents of the United States.

The endurance it takes to overcome the racism is a war that Black executives must survive. From their survival, generations will follow. But the system wears people down between the job itself and battling racism and sexism. Unfortunately, advertising is subjective and qualitative versus objective and quantitative. It's all about the customers' liking versus the actual ability to provide substantial performance. As a gymnast, one may perform perfectly, but the judges give you a 6 versus a 10 because they don't like your outfit, you, or your routine. Revisiting the corporate life of Jim Glover demonstrates how many white traditionalists promote the notion of the truth being 90% perception. Yet, Glover shows how exuding 100% perseverance despite nonsensical racism and alternative facts, one can survive and move on to greatness.

While at Leo Burnett, Jim Glover overcame the past that Needham, Harper, Steers had attempted to lock Glover into. Needham continually attacked Glover's credibility, abilities and earning capacity. From the nosy secretary telling the entire agency, top white executives slandered and shamed him, claiming he was not a good hire, nor he was he worth it to Burnett. Needham attempted to undermine Glover's rise at Leo Burnett. Yet, Glover left and went to Burnett directly. Glover continued to work on McDonald's commercials, but he wanted to work for the adult division. Glover had been the lead ad agent that worked on the most memorable commercials from McDonald's from the 1980s to the 1990s. Glover had to battle certain administrators at Leo Burnett during his tenure. They believed the "bs"-- biased slander-- that Needham had placed upon him. Nevertheless, Glover kept pushing forward even getting a white ally as a partner that was working as an art director. However, one white traditionalist from Memphis, who was a blatant racist, hired Glover's art director--the white ally, and refused to hire Glover. The "Memphis nemesis" thought that by taking Glover's partner, the art director, Glover's ability to perform would be completely impeded and destroyed, but that was far from the truth. Glover spoke to the art director. The art director stated that the team he was on didn't want to hire Glover because they believed all the racist lies started by Needham.

Glover was forced to hire another art director, but the man was not as effective as a creative; he was more of a worker-- a role player. A Black man, efficient, but not innovative. Glover wanted to work on the McDonald's adult campaign versus being excluded and placed on other McDonald's campaigns after seven years. Moreover, the company continued playing games and wouldn't make him creative director and Glover planned to leave. Then suddenly, Glover was promoted, but the "Memphis nemesis" was in management as an executive. The "Memphis nemesis" hired a white woman as the creative director. The white women he hired was one of his minions. Glover had to tolerate the creative director aka the "minion boss." Yet, Glover was given amenities and distractions. Later, he was forced to work alone without an art director.

One day, Glover left to get his wife a Christmas gift after a production meeting. Hours later, the "minion boss" called after

Glover as if he had abandoned the production. She attempted to place him on probation, claiming he walked off a shoot-- but it was actually a post-production meeting. The "minion boss" was attempting to force Glover to sign a form claiming he admitted to walking off set, even though they both knew it wasn't true. Next, Glover found himself in front of a lawyer, the "minion boss," and others in a set-up initiated by the "Memphis nemesis." The "minion boss" admitted to Glover that the "Memphis nemesis" didn't like him personally. He just didn't want a "Black" in his group.

Glover was reduced to a smaller office and his amenities were even further constrained. Glover began losing his enthusiasm altogether, yet still had victories. Yet, the fight in him had subsided. No one was looking out for him. Glover decided to quit. He was done with all of it. No one tried to stop him. Even after Glover left the agency, a white ally came to him. The white ally stated that the "minion boss" kept claiming Glover was a bum despite Glover's accomplishments and awards that he won for himself and the agency. Even the white allies weren't really allies, they simply played along to excel but they never "transitioned" to have Glover's back. Glover didn't hesitate to completely let go of the company, the position, the life. As a champion he would keep his soul, maintain his sense of self-actualization, and focus on living for his family, living for himself. Glover had a legal case but since he signed an actual silent agreement, to simply quell the situation, he couldn't do much but move on with his life.

Glover had the heart of a champion but had yet to experience being a hero who conquered adversity completely. He conquered it completely in advertising by moving forward professionally and personally. It was a matter of the champion's journey being one not of victories alone, but one of progression. Glover worked for Burrell Communications as well as well as his own agency, making him an icon of leadership, recognized by Black and non-Black advertising agencies. Glover was and remains a phoenix of American advertisers. He represents the champion that fights to keep coming back stronger from setbacks to remain relevant in the game, in the market (Shelton, 2021a).

Similar to Glover's experiences at Needham and Burnett, Chambers notes that Black professionals are rated on a different scorecard, knowing they are not given a chance to be mediocre. Mediocrity is not only a sliding scale; it is part of white privilege as it exists in corporate America. Black professionals have to perform "above the bar" raised to heights they know Blacks can't clear. However, many Black executives are viewed by white traditionalists as transient or temporary space fillers. If their performance enriches the corporation – cool, but if their performance is average, they are soon replaced. Even when Black professionals succeed, they are still forced out of their positions and transferred or worse. Many Black executives tolerate the assault and emotional war criminal behavior of white traditionalists because they feel obligated to the Black predecessors that made a way for the Black professional to continue. It's a sense of honor and obligation that many Black executives feel to the Black community as a whole, which motivates them to weather the storm. That's why building networks is paramount. The enemy is not going anywhere, so it's best to maintain a steady supply of troops to maintain the front line (Shelton, 2021c).

Black professionals keep expanding their roles, even though they have been pigeonholed into urban relations and D&I. Black people continue to spread the base by using existing platforms in which Black professionals have succeeded. Black professionals need to continue to build networks at lower costs regarding money and time, then focus on relationships with each other. By strengthening relationships with each other, Black professionals can generate

330

a force of varied skills and professionals necessary to keep Black influence and expansion moving forward (Shelton, 2021c).

According to Chambers, at the end of the day, we don't need to always have a conference or organization to network, we simply need to share information freely. It could be in a text or link in an email with information or even hard copy documents. Online meetings have become a tool of major communication due to the pandemic; therefore, when the pandemic is over, it would be best to continue using the online platforms as an inexpensive alternative to travel and lodging. Simply checking in with each other and sharing ideas can lead to a proactive period of achievement for all Black professionals involved (Shelton, 2021c).

To succeed as champions, Black people, especially Black executives, need to stop viewing each other with false divisions. For instance, we need to relinquish judgments of who has earned a degree and who has not or judging graduates of historically Black colleges and universities versus state schools or Ivy League institutions. We need to focus on how to help each other versus worrying about assisting each other and feeling we are wasting our time. We need to stop viewing assisting others from whom we don't see im-

331

mediate turnover as an imbalanced relationship. This fear keeps us from uniting as a force. We need to avoid falling prey to our own internal prejudices, inadequacies, or envy. Considering everything from colorism, bias against types of hair, body type, height, any silly surface dislike we may personally have we need to let go. By building and maintaining relationships versus cold, cliquish organizations that make various individuals feel isolated, makes a difference. Relationships allow for people with different perspectives to share because they understand all parties are valued even if there is some disagreement in approach or focus. In order for Black leadership to excel, we must engage and understand differing views and experiences as Black professionals (Shelton, 2021c).

Black people need to embrace their "Afrodiversity," the different regional aspects of various African Americans who share a common history but have a variety of experiences. From these various experiences, African Americans possess internal uniqueness and insight. Now is the time for the call to action that Black people unite and understand the need to enrich our varied sociocultural experiences in the United States. We thought society was post-racial with the election of President Barack Obama in 2008 and 2012. We thought the race wars were over, but in reality, President Obama's election to the highest seat in the Nation, revealed even more racism in various aspects that demanded attention and uncovered the battles ahead. The war is not behind us, we are still in the middle of it. The only change is the realization of how deep racism is and how many tools we have to defeat it in all aspects of American culture, specifically corporate America (Shelton, 2021c).

To keep corporations accountable, we need to make public what is private. Corporations need to be accountable for their claims of solidarity with the Black community, especially increasing Black authenticity and Black-led leadership. If Black professionals expose the truth, it forces corporations to prove they are sincere. Even if it's a matter of violating an NDA—if the NDA centers on a violation of human rights in any form or fashion. Sarbanes-Oxley protects whistleblowers from any corporate retaliation. At the end of the day, money leads to change. Black professionals must use their platforms to influence the consumer, regardless of their demographic. The consumer equals money. Once corporations feel challenged financially, they respond to the pressure to change (Shelton, 2021c).

We need to continue to push for the seats to lead with African American authenticity and internal diversity. That means we need to push to be content creators, directors, producers, videographers, casting directors, and writers. Real power in advertisement lies behind the camera and the purse strings versus simply being on screen or featured in print. We have to address multifaceted representation of African Americans in media, social media, and on other digital platforms. The sale of representation aligns the values or perspectives of customers with a certain product or service (Shelton, 2021c). However, changing customers' views depends on providing a spectrum of authentic presentations of Black people by Black people. Unfortunately, many American consumers are still swayed by the monolithic view of Black people as a single group versus the various African Americans, Caribbean Americans, and American Africans (first to third generation Americans of African descent). Therefore, the knowledge of this continued cultural denial demands that Black executives flood the table to persuade and correct the portrayal of African Americans as a whole. With greater representation, we can better offer the image and presentation the spectrum of "African America."

The advertising industry is lagging behind other industries because they are clearly rooted in white traditionalism, which reflects white supremacist values. The hidden aspect of ad agencies as a source of racial animosity is a matter of anonymity per individual agency. Basically, the brands that hire the ad agencies take the impact for investing into fallacies that ad agencies continue to manufacture and reproduce (Shelton, 2021c). Advertisement shapes all aspects of business in the public and private sectors. If white men continue to lead, American society will continue to be shaped by a narrow-minded, myopic perspective. Black leadership expands the perspective, the view, the values, and thus the audience. Advertising determines how people feel about themselves in addition to presenting them a narrative of how they are viewed by others. Consider the reversal in recent commercials where Black consumers receive service from white or other non-Black service providers. This makes African Americans feel more accepted in society not solely as service providers, but as consumers recognized for their valued business.

Hip-hop became the golden goose of American advertisement because of its marketability and has never fully been attributed to true hip hop creators who rose out of economic struggle. White people simply appropriated the music for commercial use. They look for Elvis versus Little Richard or Macklemore versus the Migos (Shelton, 2021c). White people will sacrifice the quality and authenticity of product, process, or leadership to maintain a racist relationship with other white professionals and consumers. The maintenance of the exclusive relationship is solely due to racist discomfort centered on the fact that Black people may outperform whites. Any outperformance is seen as control, and most predominantly white-led organizations are not ready to share power due to their fear of losing all of their power, influence, and eventually profit share. Many white people are not willing to "transition" from traditionalism to pluralism. Advertising is an "idea" business, but the relationships depend on how high and how far Black people can go based on relationships versus ideas alone. Therefore, the perspectives where individuals frame ideas, needs to change through proactive authentic presentations of Black people and presentations by Black professionals.

Black people have the power to impact various industries as professionals, namely marketing, entertainment, customer service, education, and politics. We just haven't used our collective power as a force. Instead, we have sacrificed collective gain for individual benefit or the sense that we are still navigating white-led leadership with no other option but self-focus, which is selfish. By having a selfish mentality, we only support the continuation of white traditionalism and remain silent by sticking with the "bs" biased situations.

Black people in all lines of industry must understand we need to get out of our own way. The greatness is in us. We simply need to tap into our majestic ingenuity and will to lead. We have to choose a path based on our skills and choices that please us versus family, friends, teachers, mentors, coworkers, or supervisors. The truth is revealed when we take on a fight with the focus of winning regardless of the twists and turns within the fight itself. We can't let our minds create monsters out of anxiety. We must take risks and embrace challenge and change. Through challenge, we expand our earning. We must focus less on what we know and more on what you don't know. It is there where we will learn (Shelton, 2021c).

The populations of the world are shifting, specifically in the U.S. where the majority of the population will be Latino and African American by 2040. The reason is based on political power which leads to legal power that influences job opportunities, community building, education, health, and food sources. This leads to population growth. The need to shift to an administration that reflects the population change has started. However, there are efforts to discontinue this flow by white traditionalists. This effort is directed at any and all weaknesses in American society that remain solely controlled by white traditionalists. As stated earlier, to solely have a monolithic white agenda as the basis of control in America has led to missed opportunities and denied excellence in exchange for mistakes and mediocrity out of fear of white populations being overran

by people of color. The latter could not be further from the truth regarding fears that many whites have as their population makes them
closer and closer to a minority in the future.

Nevertheless, the current Black professional pursuing executive positions in the corporate America, healthcare, education,
politics, and tech face a spectrum of discrimination and oppression.
However, focus on network-building and generating alliances that
promote the success of Black leadership as a force versus a few individuals who lack the true desires of the Black executive community
in mind. One of the strengths to maintain a progression of Black
leadership despite white traditionalist efforts to oppose it is focusing
on mentorships. Mentorship should be just like D&I and have our
DNA where Black professionals are mentored by and allowed to
shadow and later intern under senior Black executives and others of
color. This needs to be established and set in place with consideration of federal and state funding, as well as subsidies provided by
partnering companies such as P&G or Starbucks, who provide funding to maintain a steady flow of Black graduates, professionals, and
thus executives that will diversify and improve American commerce
and interests.

As the boxers who battle to maintain growth as champions,
they must be more focused on their destinies, rather than their dis-

tractions and focus on the present fight. We must avoid throwing don't-hit-me punches when we feel that we are tiring or weakening. We cannot fear and hesitate in analyzing, planning, implementing, and assessment of our premiere performance in regard to how we are judged in the world. We, as champions, cannot fear the judgment of those who oppose us. We know they are against us. What we must focus on is overcoming the fear of failure by maintaining our sense of team, community, movement, and progression. We cannot fear failure or the assessment thereof—the fear of repercussions under white traditionalism versus many whites who receive endless chances. We know we will change the system by flooding it, by pushing for political change, social change, judicial change. On various fronts, we will defeat the overall opposition. Yet we must not be distracted by fear.

Fear is at the root of stress. As any boxer who fights as a champion, the champion is calm and confident. The champion implements strategies and stands assertive. He or she overcomes the fear of being hit too much, the loss of confidence, the final round, the final bell then fighting not to lose versus win. The champion rises above the heart aches of stress and fear. He or she knows his or her position in the ring and knows the best strategy to outbox the opposition is to ultimately outbox fear (Atlas, 2020).

Outboxing comes from confidence and no fear. Confidence requires physical strength, speed, and balance to land punches. If you're confident enough to beat the opponent and follow through, then you will win. No matter what anyone says, the opponent will know he or she is defeated. If you don't feel like you are going to destroy your opponent, then you won't. This is the same philosophy that applies to life in general (Atlas, 2020).

To be champions, we need to be the solution with credibility and authority. The opportunities will come to us as long as we focus on building upon each other's success. We must continue to generate resources from on our accomplishments and connections thereof. We must not be afraid to toot our horn and celebrate our achievements as the master or madam of a skill, niche, or major win for the company. It's not ostentatious by honoring your own ability to perform. Get the PR you deserve. Allow no one to tell you that you are less and don't deserve it. Whether you are a corporate or entrepreneurial champion, keep grinding your way to greatness.

As a champion, you have the ability to become a reference of relevance for your company and for yourself. Take on speaking engagements, TED talks, and other events that showcase your insight and experiences. Every time you complete a task, do a press conference, write a blog, add to the company newsletter, or seek attention to be in demand and always on a crucial project. Eventually, the company will position you for the position you want. If you don't position yourself, you will forever be positioned. Position yourself through preparation. Champions perform how we prepare, and we practice for perfection. As champions, we elevate our mentality to approach challenges and overcome them. The road to becoming a champion is to become more powerful than what we overcome.

The champion has to plant his or her feet and pivot with the power of the body thrown in every punch and used in every move. Anticipate punches thrown from nowhere. The opponent will be throwing strategies or tactics that are not ethical, logical, or predictable, but are able to be defeated. When you don't know what to expect, that ambiguity can wreak havoc on your confidence. Yet, confidence is rooted in recognizing your ability to adjust in situations that demand immediate change in order to recognize the challenge, analyze it, discover resources, take action, and generate favorable resolutions. These resolutions do not have to be happy or inclusive if the opponent is not happy and inclusive. To be honest, business is a bloody battle and feelings don't pay bills.

If there is a challenge that stands before you where your feelings, your trust, your rights, or your needs have been disrespected and violated, fight with the tools and within the parameters of the battle but remember to extend your strategy even beyond the extent of the current war. Much like boxers and Civil Rights leaders of the past, much like the great orator and philosopher Frederick Douglass, James Baldwin, Fred Hampton, or Muhammad Ali would say, we might not get everything we fight for, but everything we get will be a fight.

WISDOM TO APPLY IN
THE CORPORATE RING:

• It takes endurance and strategy to become a champion, but it also takes unrelenting passion, conviction and determination. Champions fight with their minds as they fight with their fists, and when they are outmatched, they dig deeper and find fortitude in their own unwillingness to be second best.

• Corporations claim they want to change, but not enough to be significantly inclusive, incorporating Black leadership. The solidarity that corporations claim with Black consumers and professionals is embargoed and imbalanced. The corporations claim they want to change their culture, but their actions don't reflect it.

- To keep corporations accountable, we need to make public what is private. Corporations need to be accountable for their claims of solidarity with the Black community, especially increasing Black authenticity and Black-led leadership. If Black professionals expose the truth, it forces corporations to prove they are sincere.

- At the present, what is taking place regarding racial equity, especially in leadership, will be the foundation for the next generation of Black executives, deans, and presidents of the United States.

- To be champions, we need to be the solution with credibility and authority. The opportunities will come to us as long as we focus on building upon each other's success. We must continue to generate resources from on our accomplishments and connections thereof. We must not be afraid to toot our horn and celebrate our achievements as the master or madam of a skill, niche, or major win for the company.

ACKNOWLEDGMENTS

Below are my acknowledgements to my Wife, Family, Friends and team.

I have to start by thanking my awesome wife Carla Shelton for helping me get through this process and helping me get to the results. When I decided to take this on you said whatever you need I got you. So thanks for bringing me the coffee and encouragement in the morning when you knew my faith was on fumes and continuing to tell me the impossible was possible! Without you I couldn't have done it.

CONTRIBUTORS

Jim Glover
Jason Chambers
Derek Walker
Keni Thacker
Cheryl Grace
Peter Levitan
Doug Zanger
Juan Roberts

ADVISORS

DeVerges Jones
Michael Gass
Peter Levitan
Willa Robinson

"Thanks to everyone on the Wil Power team who helped me so much. Special thanks to Michael Hedges and Connie Mahoney my incredible editors for always helping me keep the vision, and Sherre Titus, my prolific proof-reader, my book coach Willa Robinson, and Juan Roberts, the dopest most gifted book cover and interior designer I could ever pray for."

FAMILY

Carla Shelton, Kiara Casillas, Marina Shelton , Ryan Shelton, Caleb Casillas, AJ Casillas and Camilla Shelton, My Mom and Dad.

REFERENCES

Armour, N. (2021, January 22) Opinion: NFL owners' only commitment to racial diversity is standing in its way. *USA Today*. Retrieved from https://amp-usatoday-com.cdn.ampproject.org/c/s/amp.usatoday.com/amp/6665646002

Atlas, T. (2021, February 15) Teddy Atlas on UFC 258 Usman win over Burns + Boxing Updates (Diaz vs Rakhimov, Warrington vs Lara, Joe Smith Jr

Babarinsa, O. (2020) Barriers to the Advancement of Black Women and Other Underrepresented Minorities on Senior and Executive Leadership Teams: A Promising Practice Study. University of Southern California, ProQuest Dissertations Publishing.

Beckwith, A.L., Carter, D.R., Peters, T., (2016) The Underrepresentation of African American Women in Executive Leadership: What's Getting in the Way? *Journal of Business Studies Quarterly*, 7(4), pp. 115-130.

Boyadzhieva, Y. (2020, June 2) "Veon settles on new chair, board members". *Mobile World Live*. Retrieved from https://www.mobileworldlive.com/featured-content/top-three/veon-settles-on-new-chair-board-members

Bradley, L. (2019, April 23) Former CBS Executive Slams the Network for Its "White Problem".
Vanity Fair Hollywood. Retrieved from https://www.vanityfair.com/hollywood/2019/04/cbs-diversity-problem-whitney-davis-essay

Brown, D. (2020, June 23) 'Keep this energy up:' Black-owned businesses see surge of interest amid racism protests. *USA Today*. Retrieved from https://www.usatoday.com/story/money/2020/06/23/black-owned-businesses-see-surge-interest-amid-race-protests/3207595001/
Brooks, K.J. (2019, December 10) Why so many black business profes-

sionals are missing from the C-suite. *CBS News*. Retrieved from https://www.cbsnews.com/news/black-professionals-hold-only-3-percent-of-executive-jobs-1-percent-of-ceo-jobs-at-fortune-500-firms-new-report-says/

Bush, J.A. (2020) Barriers to African Americans in Healthcare Leadership Attainment and the Need for Sponsorship. Northcentral University, ProQuest Dissertations Publishing, 2020. 28002888. Retrieved from https://search.proquest.com/openview/1b9e64cadf1a008dd31ac-010b0ea6ee6/1?pq-origsite=gscholar&cbl=18750&diss=y ProQuest

Caldwell, C.E. (2017) Black Lives Matter: A Corporate Conversation Worth Having? Texas State University. Honors Thesis.

Cathy Gurchieck (2021) Rosalind Brewer Becomes Third Black Woman to Head a Fortune 500 Company https://www.shrm.org/resourcesandtools/hr-topics/behavioral-competencies/global-and-cultural-effectiveness/pages/rosalind-brewer-becomes-3rd-black-woman-to-head-a-fortune-500-company.aspx

Chen, C.L. & Lucero, J.M. (2020) We Asked the Experts: Breaking the Cycle of Attrition in Perioperative Academic Medicine. *World J Surg*. Retrieved from https://doi.org/10.1007/s00268-020-05651-7

Coachman, D. (2009, June 1) Breaking the (Glass) Concrete Ceiling. *Black Enterprise*. Retrieved from https://www.blackenterprise.com/breaking-the-glass-concrete-ceiling/

Dubrovensky, T.M. (2020) The Black Religious Woman's Corporate Survival: An Independent Study of Race, Gender, Religion, and the Superwoman Schema. Indiana University. Dissertation.

Genzlinger, N. (2019, January 17) Barbara Gardner Proctor, Barrier-Breaking Ad Executive, Dies at 86. *The New York Times*. Retrieved from https://www.nytimes.com/2019/01/17/obituaries/barbara-gardner-proctor-trailblazing-ad-executive-dies-at-86.html

Glover, J. (2020, June 29) How did Blacks get into advertising anyway? *Reel Chicago*. Retrieved from https://reelchicago.com/article/how-did-blacks-get-into-advertising-anyway/

Hancock, B., Williams, M., Manyika, J., & Yee, L. (2021, February 21) Race in the workplace: The Black experience in the US private sector. McKinsey & Company. Retrieved from https://www.mckinsey.com/featured-insights/diversity-and-inclusion/race-in-the-workplace-the-black-experience-in-the-us-private-sector

Hartman, H. (2021, January 12) The Case of Cheryl Grace Typifies Corporate Racism. *N'Digo*. Retrieved from https://ndigo.com/2021/01/12/the-case-of-cheryl-grace-typifies-corporate-racism/

Grace (2021, March 22) The lawsuit alleged Cheryl Grace hit a glass ceiling on the climb up the corporate ladder, when Nielsen passed over her for an expanded role. https://www.chicagotribune.com/business/ct-biz-nielsen-lawsuit-discrmination-settlement-20210322-tmjxie7fevbe3i56aeqh7mvw34-story.html

James, M. (2021, January 24) Inside CBS' fraught investigation into allegations of racism and misogyny. *Los Angeles Times*. Retrieved from https://www.latimes.com/entertainment-arts/business/story/2021-01-24/cbs-television-stations-peter-dunn-racism-sexism

Massie, V.M. (2016, June 23) White women benefit most from affirmative action — and are among its fiercest opponents. *Vox*. Retrieved from https://www.vox.com/2016/5/25/11682950/fisher-supreme-court-white-women-affirmative-action

McCall, N. (2020, November 23) Black Americans are forced to operate our entire lives in battle mode. It's utterly exhausting. *The Washington Post* Retrieved from https://www.washingtonpost.com/graphics/2020/national/george-floyd-america/nathan-mccall-systemic-racism-higher-education/?fbclid=IwAR2S6f56Js39cHFR362WxuwMD7EHgo_FXYSaK-WBeskzYSS0bI22xZWDfewQ

McQueen, L.S Leadership in Corporate America. Trevecca Chasing the C-Suite: The Lived Experiences of African American Women Who Pursue Executive Nazarene University, ProQuest Dissertations Publishing, 2020, p. 4, 5.

Miller, S. (2020, June 11) Black Workers Still Earn Less than Their White Counterparts. SHRM. Retrieved from https://www.shrm.org/resourcesandtools/hr-topics/compensation/pages/racial-wage-gaps-persistence-poses-challenge.aspx

My Black Receipt (2020) "About Us." *My Black Receipt.* Retrieved from https://www.myblackreceipt.com/about-us/

Raton, T.S. (2012, February 11) Young, Gifted and Black Series: African American youth invents surgical technique at age 14. *Milwaukee Courier.* Retrieved from https://milwaukeecourieronline.com/index.php/2012/02/11/african-american-youth-invents-surgical-technique-at-age-14

Risen, C. (2016, June 25) Jack Daniel's Embraces a Hidden Ingredient: Help from a Slave. *The New York Times.* Retrieved from https://www.nytimes.com/2016/06/26/dining/jack-daniels-whiskey-nearis-green-slave.html

Roberts, L.M. & Mayo, A.J. (2019, November 14) Toward a Racially Just Workplace: Diversity efforts are failing black employees. Here's a better approach. *HBR.* Retrieved from https://hbr.org/2019/11/toward-a-racially-just-workplace

Shamira, I. (2020, June 23) Netflix's 'Strong Black Lead' Marketing Team Shows the Power (and Business Benefit) of Amplifying Black Voices. *USA Today.* Retrieved from https://www.usatoday.com/story/money/2020/06/23/black-owned-businesses-see-surge-interest-amid-race-protests/3207595001/

Showtime (Feb 1, 2021) "Wu-Tang Clan: Of Mics and Men: Episode 4 (TVMA)". Showtime Documentaries. Retrieved from https://www.youtube.com/watch?v=yvSmPs4Q-gY

Sisco, S. (2020, August 20) Race-conscious career development: Exploring self-preservation and coping strategies of Black professionals in corporate America. *SAGE*, 22(4), pp. 419-436.

Statista (n.d.) Gross domestic product (GDP) of the United States at current prices from 1984 to 2021. Retrieved from https://www.statista.com/statistics/263591/gross-domestic-product-gdp-of-the-united-states/

Taha, K.M. (2020, June 26) Dear Advertising, I'm Still Worried About the White Elephants in The Room. *Dear Advertising*. Retrieved from https://medium.com/@kifayamtaha/dear-advertising-im-still-worried-about-the-white-elephants-in-the-room-b0659ca4cb62

Tucker, J. (2017, November 13) The Road To $1.5 Trillion In Black Buying Power and Dispelling A Common Myth. *Black Enterprise*. Retrieved from https://www.blackenterprise.com/the-road-to-1-5-trillion-in-black-buying-power/

Wachowski, L. & Wachowski, L. (2003) The Matrix Reloaded. Burbank, CA: Warner Bros.

Yancy, G. (2016). *Black Bodies, White Gazes*. New York: Rowman & Littlefield.

Zheng, Lily (2020, June 15) We're Entering the Age of Corporate Social Justice. *HBR*. Retrieved from https://hbr.org/2020/06/were-entering-the-age-of-corporate-social-justice